The Mark of Discipleship

MARTINS OKONKWO

WESTBOW°
PRESS
A DIVISION OF THOMAS NELSON
& ZONDERVAN

Scripture taken from the New King James Version. Copyright 1979, 1980, 1982 by Thomas Nelson, inc. Used by permission. All rights reserved.

Scripture taken from the King James Version of the Bible.

All scriptural quotations are from the King James, the New King James, and the Good News versions of the Bible.

Cover Page Designs reference: www.wallcoo.com

WestBow Press books may be ordered through booksellers or by contacting:

WestBow Press
A Division of Thomas Nelson & Zondervan
1663 Liberty Drive
Bloomington, IN 47403
www.westbowpress.com
1 (866) 928-1240

ISBN: 978-1-4908-2763-6 (sc)
ISBN: 978-1-4908-2765-0 (hc)
ISBN: 978-1-4908-2764-3 (e)

Library of Congress Control Number: 2014903857

Printed in the United States of America.

WestBow Press rev. date: 2/26/2014

Contents

The Mark of Discipleship aims to open our understanding of the real meaning and scope of the divine task of drawing and winning a lost and directionless world to God through painstaking and costly sacrifices.

This book helps highlight the positive roles divine grace, wisdom, prophecy, prayer, and the Holy Spirit play in doing the discipleship work of the kingdom of God. It also restates the compelling need for both quality control and urgency in the course of finishing this huge task of discipleship.

The Mark of Discipleship offers biblical and contemporary models to help the church effectively build this great kingdom work of discipleship.

It is compelling reading.

The Great Commission

Go ye therefore, and teach all nations, baptizing them
in the name of the Father, and of the Son, and of
the Holy Ghost: Teaching them to observe all things
whatsoever I have commanded you: and, lo, I am with
you always, even unto the end of the world, amen.
—Matthew 28:19–2

Foreword

Discipleship—the making of disciples, is central to the divine functions of the church of God. It was the main work our Lord Jesus Christ paid priority attention to while he was on earth. He placed greater emphasis on quality discipleship and passed on this hunger, drive, and desire to his disciples and by extension the church he built.

To him, his food was to do or finish his Father's work, and he consistently stressed he had work to accomplish.

> In the mean while his disciples prayed him, saying, Master, eat. But he said unto them, I have meat to eat that ye know not of. Therefore said the disciples one to another, Hath any man brought him ought to eat? Jesus saith unto them, My meat is to do the will of him that sent me, and to finish his work. (John 4:31–34)

Friends, discipleship is paramount in God's priorities for mankind and commands our total obedience to his divine will. Jesus' unwavering commitment and urgency to faithfully finish the work of heavenly discipleship the Father gave him underlines the importance God places on quality discipleship.

All that the Father giveth me shall come to me; and him that cometh to me I will in no wise cast out. For I came down from heaven, not to do mine own will, but the will of him that sent me. And this is the Father's will which hath sent me, that of all which he hath given me I should lose nothing, but should raise it up again at the last day. (John 6:37–39)

I have glorified thee on the earth: I have finished the work which thou gavest me to do. (John 17:4)

This book will open our understanding to the real meaning and scope of the noble task of winning the world over to God through the Great Commission Jesus gave to his church in Matthew 28. It presents discipleship as making and multiplying followers of Jesus and his soon-coming eternal kingdom empowered by the Holy Spirit, the divine dynamo of God's kingdom.

Go ye therefore, and teach all nations, baptizing them in the name of the Father, and of the Son, and of the Holy Ghost: Teaching them to observe all things whatsoever I have commanded you: and, lo, I am with you always, even unto the end of the world. Amen. (Matthew 28:19–20)

The Mark of Discipleship goes a step further by highlighting the prominent roles divine grace, wisdom, prophecy, and prayer play in accomplishing this great and noble work of the kingdom given to the church. It also stresses the need for quality control and urgency in finishing this great task of the Great Commission. It opens up a new challenge to the church of God to evolve ways of engaging in dialogue a hurting and darkness-prone world and in the process win it over to God.

This challenge must be confronted head-on without losing but retaining its unique nature. *The Mark of Discipleship* suggests biblical and contemporary models that can help the church of God effectively accomplish this noble kingdom work of discipleship.

God bless as you leaf through the pages of this Holy Spirit–inspired volume.

Pastor Martins Okonkwo

CHAPTER 1

What Discipleship Is

Behold, I will send for many fishers saith the Lord,
and they shall fish them; and after will I send for many
hunters, and they shall hunt them from every mountain,
and from every hill, and out of the holes of the rocks.
—Jeremiah 16:16

Discipleship can be defined as the ministry of multiplication or divine spreading. It is the art of fishing for or harvesting lost souls for the kingdom of God for divine restoration and enduring fellowship with God. Discipleship is the training and equipping of men and women under the divine guidance and leading of the Spirit of God for divine service to God and humanity. This involves the systemic, programmed art of following our Savior, Jesus Christ, who has promised us earthly blessings and eternal life with him and the Father in heaven. It involves a selfless service or commitment as represented by a total submission, total consecration, of the self for servanthood.

And he saith unto them, follow me, and I will make
you fishers of men. And they straightway left their
nets, and followed him. And going on from thence,

> he saw other two brethren, James the son of Zebedee,
> and John his brother in a ship with Zebedee their
> father, mending their nets: and he called them; And
> they immediately left the ship and their father and
> followed him. (Matthew 4:19–22)

Friends, discipleship demands total surrender and consecration or submission to he who has called you into servant hood; No half measure is acceptable. Note that in the aforementioned passage, the first four sets of disciples left all they had—fathers, nets, fish, and wealth—to follow him. This explains why Jesus asked us, as chosen disciples, to leave all and follow him.

> He that loveth father and mother more than me is
> not worthy of me; and he that loveth son or daughter
> more than me is not worthy of me; and he that taketh
> not his cross and followeth me, is not worthy of me.
> (Matthew 10:38, 39)

The reason for discipleship is that only disciples of Christ will enter the kingdom of heaven. God wants everyone to be saved, programmed, and set for eternal glory as well as discipled into his glorious heaven.

This is why, and importantly so, God wants us to be well and fully trained in the art and manner of heavenly discipline, character, holiness, wisdom, and nature before we can enter into his holy heaven to worship and serve him forever.

The blood covenant of salvation has paved the way for our discipleship into heaven; it is the last master card God has finally used to call his people into discipleship. However, it is imperative to stress that only few among the called will eventually be chosen for eternal life in heaven. A divine life of perpetual bliss. This implies that only those who genuinely respond to this discipleship call will pass the litmus test and qualify for entrance into heaven.

> So the last shall be the first, and the first last; for many
> be called, but few chosen. (Matthew 20:16)

What Jesus is implying here is that only well-trained Christian believers will see his Father in heaven. This is the mark of discipleship or the ministry of divine multiplication.

Discipleship has its central focus on global evangelism and was the original concept and vision of its author and finisher, our Lord. The global vision was to multiply faithful disciples with the imparted life of Christ, who would in turn teach and pass on this art to others. This explains the reason for the Great Commission as handed down to the apostles and the disciples of old and that has been passed on to our own generation for onward transmission.

> Go ye therefore, and teach all nations, baptizing them
> in the name of the Father, and of the Son and of the
> Holy Ghost; teaching them to observe all the things
> what so ever I have commanded you; and lo, I am
> with you always, even unto the end of the world;
> Amen. (Matthew 28:19–20)

Teaching others or committing the doctrines of Jesus Christ is the hallmark or rallying point of disciplining men and women into the kingdom of God. Teaching, or committing, involves the deliberate art of a deep-rooted transmission of Christlike life from one to another, as can be seen in the case of Paul and Timothy.

> Hold fast the form of sound words which thou hast heard of me, in faith, and love which is in Christ Jesus. That good thing [the sound doctrines of Jesus] which was committed unto thee keep by the Holy Ghost which dwelleth in us. (2 Timothy 1:13–14)

In 2 Timothy 2, Paul admonished his son in the Lord, Timothy, to transmit to others all Paul had committed into his life for increased discipleship and unpolluted fellowship.

> And the things that thou hast heard of me among many witnesses, the same commit thou to faithful men, who shall be able to teach others also. (2 Timothy 2:2)

Friends, God has redeemed us with the precious blood of Jesus Christ for enduring discipleship. He wants us to go to all nations and win souls into his kingdom through the divine art of Spirit-led discipleship.

Have we met this expectation of our heavenly Father? Why is the body of Christ, the church, in a spiritual coma? Why does the church of God on earth revolve in a circle? A cursory look at the churches on earth today reveals that we are far from meeting this divine expectation. The spirit of unfaithfulness has taken hold of the body of Christ.

Much noise has been made by some of these churches about evangelism, fellowship programs, and doctrines, but no noticeable, positive effect has manifested itself of such wasted human efforts and resources. The church has left out its first love, Jesus, from its programming, planning, and leading and thus has brought in its wake pronounced decline and decadence. We have neglected the owner of the church and his Holy Spirit, which reveals and releases revelation for the growth and faith of the church. The Holy Spirit has been relegated to the background.

For continued and faithful discipleship, Jesus promised to send a comforter who would teach us all things on how to be effective and truly resourceful in our discipleship programs.

> But the comforter which is the Holy Ghost, whom the father will send in my name, he shall teach you all things and bring all things to your remembrance, whatsoever I have said unto you. (John 14:26)

Are we allowing this precious, divine gift—the Holy Spirit—to perform his functions in the church, or has he been boxed into a tight corner? Until we destroy the enticing wisdom of man and the doctrinal perversities in our churches today and allow the enthronement of the multifaceted wisdom of God as revealed to us by the Holy Spirit, the church will for a long time remain in a deplorable state of spiritual coma, docility, and unfaithfulness.

Friends, the parable of the sower Jesus Christ narrated to his disciples in Matthew 13 presents laudable lessons on how to put in perspective the real model of approved heavenly disciples expected of the church. In this model of discipleship, Jesus showed the unique importance the Word of God plays in fashioning an acceptable model of heavenly discipleship. He presented the infallible Word of God as a very useful seed that produces and sustains true discipleship.

> But one thing is needful: and Mary hath chosen that good part, which shall not be taken away from her. (Luke 10:42)

A seed represents a compressed life that reproduces further life. A seed, as small as it looks, contains all the character, nature, and vitality of individual life. The Word of God represents the spiritual seed that changes and transforms sinful lives and transfers Christ's life of holiness, purity, faithfulness, and complete obedience to these changed lives. Jesus is that Word of God, which by implication represents the spiritual seed.

Scriptural Search: John 1:1–4, 14; Revelation 19:13.

In the parable of the sower, we are reminded that the regenerative power of God's Word transforms, cleanses, prepares, and thus qualifies people for entrance into the kingdom. This explains why Jesus told Martha in Luke 10 that the Word of God should be desired more than anything else.

Scriptural Search: "But one thing is needful: and Mary hath chosen that good part, which shall not be taken away from her"(Luke 10:42; Psalm 119:9, 11, 105, 120; John 15:3; Ephesians 5:26–27; Ezekiel 36:25–26).

Jesus told Pastor Nicodemus that a person must be born again by the water of God's Word and the power of the Holy Spirit before entrance into heaven would be guaranteed by God.

> There was a man of the Pharisees, named Nicodemus, a ruler of the Jews: The same came to Jesus by night, and said unto him, Rabbi, we know that thou art a teacher come from God: for no man can do these miracles that thou does, except God be with him. Jesus answered and said unto him, Verily, verily, I say unto thee, Except a man be born again, he cannot see the kingdom of God. Nicodemus saith unto him, How can a man be born when he is old? Can he enter the second time into his mother's womb, and be born? Jesus answered, Verily, verily, I say unto thee, Except a man be born of water and of the Spirit, he cannot enter into the kingdom of God. (John 3:1–5)

Brethren, the Word of God is an everlasting spiritual seed that saves and sustains us here on earth and in heaven. It introduces us to the family of God as well as prepares us for heaven. It is as important to Christian believers as are to farmers. Farmland is useless without good, life-reproducing seeds.

Scriptural Search: Psalm 119:89; Matthew 24:35; Isaiah 40:8; Luke 16:17; 1 John 2:17.

The following lessons can be learned from the biblical narrative of the sower.

1. The wayside model of discipleship

This type of discipleship is the shallow kind in which distractions and lack of depth of teaching, pastoral care, and follow-up in some of our churches gives the Devil and his agents the opportunity to destroy the newfound faith of some Christian believers. This is exemplified in the narrative Jesus gave about the man delivered of unclean spirits who lacked the Word of God due to inadequate teachings and pastoral care, counsel, love, and fellowship.

> When the unclean spirit is gone out of a man, he walketh through dry places, seeking rest; and finding none, he saith, I will return unto my house whence I came out. And when he cometh, he findeth it swept and garnished. Then goeth he, and taketh to him seven other spirits more wicked than himself; and they enter in, and dwell there: and the last state of that man is worse than the first. (Luke 11:24–26)

The church, therefore, needs to be careful and more detailed in its teaching, preaching, pastoral counseling, and other discipleship programs to properly teach and disciple the people of God to avoid the lurking wolves devouring the faith of God's children.

> I am the good shepherd: the good shepherd giveth his life for the sheep. (John 10:11)

> Be sober, be vigilant; because your adversary the devil, as a roaring lion, walketh about, seeking whom he may devour: Whom resist steadfast in the faith,

knowing that the same afflictions are accomplished in your brethren that are in the world. (1 Peter 5:8–9)

Scriptural Search: Acts 6:1–6; John 21:15–17.

2. The quicksand (stony) model of discipleship

This is the kind of tailored Christian discipleship in which new and old disciples of Christ leave the narrow way to heaven because of persecution and tribulation in this evil world. This is because they were not well built up in Christ and his doctrines and commands.

Their primary focus is on miracles, healing, deliverance, and other material things of this world. These people were not properly founded on the major Christian foundations of holiness, righteousness, true repentance, obedience, love, and faithfulness, among others. Training converts properly based on priceless Christian foundations would help root their Christian faith and hope in Christ's finished work of Calvary and thus guarantee their eternal life. Jesus condemned the scribes and Pharisees for reproducing half-baked disciples after crisscrossing the world, searching for disciples. He accused them of increasing the chances of these disciples going to hell rather than heaven. In our present world, similar things are happening. People and churches conduct crusades and other Christian fellowships and focus people's attention on signs and wonders, prosperity, and material things that end on earth rather than pointing them toward heaven.

It is very dangerous to train disciples on quicksand, get-rich-quick kinds of ideals; this makes them put their minds on earthly things rather than on love, affection, and heaven. The Spirit of God calls the church to stop these quicksand programs and resort to the original apostolic and prophetic blueprints Jesus gave the early church by quickly reprogramming their discipleship programs to conform to those Christian foundations Jesus built the church on.

Scriptural Search: Amos 8:11–12, 9:11–13.

3. The thorn bush model of discipleship

This is the kind of discipleship in which the cares, lusts, and deceptions of worldly systems and fashions captivate and tempt Christian believers out of the narrow way to heaven. The choking influence of these evil, worldly things has destroyed their Christian faith and hope in the eternal life Jesus Christ has prepared for all who obey.

4. The fertile or fruitful model of discipleship

This was the divinely approved model of discipleship Jesus Christ offered to his church while here on earth. It produces divine fruits that grant Christian believers entrance into heaven. In this model of discipleship, believers' hearts are fertile, clean, ready, and conducive for spiritual reproduction to take place between the Word of God and the Holy Spirit. The fallow or stony parts of the heart are broken and softened for the Word of God to operate effectively.

> Sow to yourselves in righteousness, reap in mercy;
> break up your fallow ground: for it is time to seek
> the LORD, till he come and rain righteousness upon
> you. (Hosea 10:12)

This process of spiritual synthesis produces in abundance the required fruit of the Spirit—love, peace, joy, faithfulness, patience, kindness, goodness, humility, and self-control that earn us respectable, glorious places in heaven.

> But the fruit of the Spirit is love, joy, peace, longsuffering, gentleness, goodness, faith, Meekness, temperance: against such there is no law. (Galatians 5:22–23)

The greater the volume of the Word of God and the readiness to assimilate and retain it, the greater the intensity to produce more fruits that lead to everlasting life.

> Deep calleth unto deep at the noise of thy waterspouts: all thy waves and thy billows are gone over me. (Psalm 42:7)

We must therefore be willing and ready, more than ever before, to cleanse and prepare our hearts to receive and retain the Word of God and the Holy Spirit for effective Christian discipleship and fruit bearing. That way, we will be fully built up in Christ and conform to the full, rapture-ready image and nature of Christ before his much-trumpeted return.

Brethren, this is the only way to assume the righteousness and holiness of God, our Father and Savior. Make your body the holy temple of God, and keep it pure till Jesus Christ returns with his rewards. In the end time, God will release the anointing for the end-time harvest via a programmed divine art of a new-age apostolic discipleship.

In March 1996, the Lord spoke to me. This revelation opened up part of God's end-time prophetic agenda: "Son, I have destined you for prosperity and world evangelism." A few months later, he spoke to me again, that time with an accompanying Scripture to go all over the world to raise people for the end-time programs of his kingdom, promising his anointed backing, financially and spiritually. His exact word as was given to me in Joel 3 was,

> Proclaim ye this amongst the gentles: prepare war, wake up mighty man. Let all the men of war draw near; let them come up: put ye in the sickle, for the harvest is ripe; come, get you down for the press is full, the vats overflow for their wickedness is great. (Joel 3:9, 12)

Friends, God is about to do a new thing in regard to commissioning and discipling men and women into his kingdom; he has released the end-time anointing for a revival that will shake the world. This will remove all religious and doctrinal precedents. Emphasis will be shifted to this great revival, which will produce discipleship unprecedented in the history of the church. It will be a tornado that blows away the old chips and enthrones a new apostolic order for end-time discipleship.

In the light of above revelation, God has declared 1996 a year of divine planting, a year of discipleship geared toward massive global evangelism. It is a year of massive repentance and turn around for God's children. Friends, this is new and crucial; it demands serious concern. God spoke prophetically through Jeremiah in connection with the birth of this end-time discipleship.

Behold I will send for many fishers [disciples], saith
the Lord and they shall fish them: and after will I send
for many hunters and they shall hunt them from every
mountain and from every hill, and out of the holes of
the rocks. (Jeremiah 16:16)

Friends, be prepared for surprises from this year 1996 onward. So
many unbelievers will, through the divine art of discipleship, be
converted to Christ all over the world no matter where they are
hiding in holes, in pits of sin, and they will be discipled properly
into the kingdom of God. Watch out for the fulfillment of this
prophecy. When he speaks, he brings it to pass. The effects and
rewards of this year of divine planting or discipleship will begin to
manifest after 2000.

Friends, this is prophetic, and no gate of hell shall prevail against it.
Be prepared for this challenge; wake up, put on your strength, and
start a planting program for the Lord in the vineyard. Ask the Lord
to use you in this new apostolic order to bring into his kingdom as
many as are lost in the world.

CHAPTER 2

Who Is a Disciple?
Qualities and Functions

By this shall all men know that ye are my
disciples if ye have love for one another.
—John 13:35

A true disciple is a sanctified, committed, and faithful follower
of Christ and his doctrines. He represents the Lord on earth and
continues his work. The Greek word for disciple is *mathetes* and means
"learner," "pupil," or "student." This implies that the congregation
of God's church on earth is a collection of dedicated and forward-
looking students who gather often to receive the divine commands
and instructions of God and the Bible, the authentic spiritual manual
for lifelong learning. A disciple is a collaborator with the Lord in the
vineyard.

For we are God's fellow workers; you are God's field,
you are God's building. (1 Corinthians 3:9)

Then saith he unto his disciples, the harvest truly is
plenteous, but the laborers are few; pray ye therefore

the Lord of the harvest that he will send forth laborers into his harvest. (Matthew 9:37–38)

The harvest above represents the multitude of lost sinners outside the kingdom, so his compassionate desire for his heavenly Father to make more disciples who will harvest these lost souls into God's kingdom.

But when he saw the multitudes, he was moved with compassion on them, because they fainted and were scattered abroad, as sheep having no shepherd. (Matthew 9:36)

Disciples are therefore supposed to be efficient ambassadors or representatives of Christ Jesus and thus efficient fruit bearers. One noticeable fruit they are expected to bear is true divine love, and this distinguishes them from the crowd.

Here is my father glorified that ye bear much fruit so shall ye be my disciples. As the father hath loved me, so have I loved you; continue ye in my love; and ye also shall bear witness, because ye have been with me from the beginning. (John 15:8, 9, 27)

Kinds of Disciples

Three major classes of disciples are easily discernible, and they play complementary roles in the ministry of divine multiplication, discipleship. These classes of disciples include apostolic, prophetic, and what can best be called missionary.

Apostolic Disciples

Apostolic disciples are those specially called, ordained, and commissioned by the Lord to deliver specific messages and make disciples of men and women who in turn will be collaborators in his vineyard harvests. They are extraordinarily called and equipped, and they have divine anointing, protection, and provisions to meet the expectations of the Lord's Great Commission.

> Ye have not chosen me, but I have chosen you and ordained you, that ye should go and bring forth fruit and that your fruit should remain: that whatsoever ye shall ask of the father in my name, he may give it you. (John 15:16)

The first apostolic disciples ordained by Jesus were the twelve apostles. They were divinely commissioned to make other disciples by teaching, healing, and setting captives free from Satan's works. They preached repentance and made disciples for the kingdom. They didn't preach prosperity, as some of us who are confused, hungry, and beggarly do today. The Master's message was repentance unto salvation, which has all the antecedents of God's holiness and righteousness. Friends, this is the Master's good news to the world.

> And He opened their understanding, that they might comprehend the Scriptures. Then He said to them, "Thus it is written, and thus it was necessary for the Christ to suffer and to rise from the dead the third day, and that repentance and remission of sins should be preached in His name to all nations, beginning

at Jerusalem. And you are witnesses of these things. Behold, I send the Promise of My Father upon you; but tarry in the city of Jerusalem until you are endued with power from on high." (Luke 24:45–49)

And when he had called unto him his twelve disciples; he gave them power against unclean spirits to cast them out and to heal all manner of sickness and all manner of diseases. Now the names of the twelve apostles are these: the first is Simon who is called Peter, and Andrew his brother; James the son of Zebedee and John his brother; Philip and Bartholomew; Thomas and Matthew the publican; James the son of Apphaeus and Lebbaeus whose surname was (Thaddaous); Simon the Canaanite, and Judas Iscariot, who also betrayed Him. These twelve Jesus sent forth and commanded them saying, go not into the way of the gentiles and into any city of the Samaritan enter ye not; but go rather to the last sheep of Israel. Heal the sick, cleanse the lepers, raise the dead, cast out devils, freely ye have received, freely give. (Matthew 10:1–6, 8)

Apostolic disciples are divinely commissioned as master builders and forerunners in the art of discipleship. They are pacesetters and special messengers of God mandated to broaden the scope of discipleship on earth.

According to the grace of God which is giving on to me, as a master builder, I have laid the foundation, and another buildeth thereon. But let every man take heed how he buildeth thereupon; for other foundations can no man lay than that is laid, which is Christ Jesus. (1 Corinthians 3:10–11)

Jesus commissioned the twelve apostolic disciples and gave them special powers to heal and set captives free through preaching repentance and salvation to men and women held captive by the enemy. The apostle Paul commenting on this special apostolic grace granted him by the Lord.

> According to the Grace of God which is given unto me as a master builder, I have laid the foundation and another buildeth there on. But let every man take head how he buildeth thereupon; for other foundation can no man lay than that is laid, which is Christ Jesus. (1 Corinthians 3:10–11)

> Then he called his twelve disciples together and gave them power and authority over all devils and to cure diseases. And He sent them to preach the Kingdom of God and to heal the sick. And they departed and went through the towns, preaching the Gospel and healing everywhere. And the apostles [the apostolic disciples], when they were returned, told him all that they had done. And he took them, and went aside privately into a desert place belonging to the city called Bethsaida. (Luke 9:1, 2, 6, 10)

The apostolic disciples had to return to the Lord for an infilling and updating after each exploit; they had to resort to a "desert place," a position of deeper consecration, fellowship, and communion. The branch cannot bear fruit except when it abides in the vine.

The apostolic discipleship programs of the church will assume a greater and glorious dimension only when this divine order is strictly followed.

> Abide in me and I in you. As the branch cannot bear
> fruit of itself except it abides in the vine: no more can
> ye, except ye abides in me. (John 15:4)

Apostolic disciples are planters of churches and other divine structures of God that expand his kingdom on earth.

> I have planted, Apollos watered; but God gave the
> increase. (1 Corinthians 3:6)

God declared the year 1999 and beyond a time of divine planting, a time of massive repentance and great apostolic, prophetic, and missionary discipleship. It is a new dawn of the new-age apostolic order. Pray that God will enlist you into this prophetic program of his, this end time.

Prophetic Disciples

These represent disciples divinely commissioned by God to receive his prophetic blueprints for the building of this new-age apostolic discipleship order. The discipleship program of every ministry must have a divine master plan from heaven for it to achieve resounding success; if not, every human effort will be wasted.

> Except the Lord build the house, they labour in vain
> that build it; except the Lord keep the city, the watch
> man waketh but in vain. (Psalm 127:1)

This work belongs to God, not humanity. It is therefore God's good pleasure to present master plans for this work to progress. Just as an architect hands building plans to a contractor that contain specifications for a perfect job, so God presents his plans to the prophetic disciples for transmission to apostolic disciples, the master builders or planters. They take the blueprints of God and make them available to the house of God, the church.

Jesus ascended into heaven and gave different gifts and offices of calling to many to continue and increase discipleship and the perfection of the saints, the spiritual church of God on earth.

> Wherefore he saith, when he ascended up on high,
> he led captivity captive, and gave gifts unto men; and
> he gave some apostles; and some prophets; and some
> evangelists; and some pastors and teachers; for the
> perfecting of saints, for the work of the ministry, for
> the edifying [strengthening] of the body of Christ.
> (Ephesians 4:8, 11, 12)

Isaiah's prophetic discipleship greatly affected all humanity; he received a genuine prophetic blueprint of salvation for mankind from the Lord. He preached repentance, restoration, and salvation of the kingdom to the backsliding people of his days. He discipled so many into God's kingdom through his prophecy. Thousands of years later, his prophecy gave birth to a new prophetic and apostolic order that ushered in our Savior, Jesus, who came with salvation and reformed discipleship.

> For unto us a child is born, unto us a son is given: and the government shall be upon his shoulder, and his name shall be called wonderful, counsellor, the mighty God, the everlasting father, the prince of peace; of the increase of his government and peace there shall be no end, upon the throne of David, and upon his Kingdom to order it and to establish it with judgment. (Isaiah 9:6–7)

The endless increase of his government and peace implies the ministry of divine multiplication, discipleship, of this new-age apostolic order we are currently in. The apostle Luke presented the fulfillment of this prophecy.

> And they came with haste, and found Mary, Joseph and the baby lying in a manger; and when they had seen it they made known abroad the saying which was told them concerning this child; for mine eyes have seen thy salvation. (Luke 2:16, 17, 30)

John the Baptist was another prophetic disciple God used to perfect the prophetic birth of the new discipleship order that heralded his salvation program for mankind. God handed down his prophetic blueprint to John the Baptist, who went on a massive discipleship program that saw the emergence of faithful disciples into the kingdom. He preached repentance and salvation to the people of his days without reservation, and in the process, he brought many into God's kingdom.

> In those days came John the Baptist, preaching in the wilderness of Judea: saying, repent ye, for the Kingdom of heaven is at hand: Then went out to him Jerusalem, and all Judea, and all the region round about Jordan, and were baptised of him in Jordan, confessing their sins. (Matthew 3:1, 2, 5, 6)

The effect of John the Baptist's discipleship was the emergence of missionary disciples who went about with faithfulness and made disciples of men and women through a conscious act of preaching repentance. He made committed disciples who followed him till his death before some joined the discipleship program of Jesus Christ. They were with him even while he was in prison.

> And John calling unto him two of his disciples sent them to Jesus saying art thou he that should come? Or look we for another? (Luke 7:19)

Missionary Disciples

These are disciples the Lord commissions with a divine mandate to reach out to the larger segments of the world to train men and women into the kingdom of God. They have been mandated to preach repentance and salvation to lost souls. The evangelists, pastors, teachers, and other church workers are in this category. They are to work hand in hand with apostolic and prophetic disciples for the expansion of God's kingdom on earth through missionary outreach programs. Such outreach programs could be open-field crusades or outreach ministries for Christian literature with the sole aim of producing and distributing tracts, books, magazines, films, and so on.

"Missionary" implies reaching out to the lost with the specific divine mission of effective soul winning or discipleship. These missionary outreach programs may be carried out locally or internationally. Right now, the Spirit of the new apostolic age is calling the unreached locally and internationally.

Just as the Lord sent forth seventy missionary disciples, he is busy sending out many others into the field. God is still calling, ordaining, and sending forth yielded vessels who will carry out the discipleship program of this new-age apostolic dispensation. The harvest is fully ripe and wasting due to few quality and effective laborers available.

> After these things the Lord appointed other seventy also, and sent them two and two before his face into every city and place, whither he himself would come; therefore said he unto them, the harvest truly is great, but the labourers are few; pray ye therefore, the Lord of the harvest, that he would send forth labourers into his harvest. (Luke 10:1–2)

Missionary disciples water what apostolic disciples have founded and planted; they are the follow-up agents who help the plants, the new converts, establish roots in the faith through outreach programs with divine backup. The apostle Paul made this revelation clearer when he wrote,

> I have planted, Apollos watered; but the Lord gave the increase now he that planted and he that watereth are one; and every man shall receive his own reward according to his own labour. (1 Corinthians 3:6, 8)

Paul and Apollos in the above passage represent two types of disciples; Paul building or planting, and Apollos watering or reaching out for deeper fellowship in the faith. Both complement each other in expanding God's kingdom on earth.

Qualities of a Disciple

The life of a true disciple is committed and programmed. Disciples must possess the following qualities.

1. Boldness

Disciples must be strong and bold enough to meet up with the challenges of doing exploits for the Lord. They must never be afraid to execute the programs of the kingdom, for God has not given us over to fear.

> For God hath not given us the Spirit of fear but of power and love and a sound mind. (2 Timothy 1:7)

The prophet Daniel, lending credence to this revelation, advised the disciples of the Lord,

> But the people [disciples] that do know their God shall be strong and do exploits. (Daniel 11:32b)

Solomon wrote concerning this as well.

> The wicked flee when no man pursueth: but the righteous are bold as a lion. (Proverbs 28:1)

Friends, the end-time discipleship is for lion-hearted disciples as prophesied by the prophet Joel; it is not for babies. You must gird your loins and be strong in the faith so the end-time power of discipleship will flow through you unhindered.

> A great people and strong; there hath not been ever the like, neither shall be any more after it, even to the years of many generations: they shall run like mighty men; they shall climb the wall like men of war; and they shall march everyone on his ways, and they shall not break their ranks. (Joel 2:2, 7)

This is a daring quality an end-time disciple must possess.

2. Willingness to Sacrifice

Disciples must be ready to make sacrifices to the point of defending the gospel even unto death. They must never compromise the truth.

> They shall put you out of the synagogues; yea, the
> time cometh, that whosoever killeth you will think
> that he doeth God service. But these things have
> I told you that when the time shall come, ye may
> remember that I told you of them. (John 16:2, 4)

The apostle Paul made painful sacrifices to preach the gospel given
to him by God to the disciples made through him. For him, to live
was Christ and to die was gain.

> We are troubled on every side, yet not distressed; we
> are perplexed but not in despair. (2 Corinthians 4:8)

Jesus said that unless we carry our cross and make sacrifices for the
kingdom, we are not his disciples (Matthew 10:31–39).

3. Humility

Disciples must be humble and ready to obey the commandments of
Jesus, who has called them into discipleship.

> Therefore, the prisoner of the lord, beseech you
> that ye walk worthy of the vocation where with ye
> are called; with lowliness and meekness [humility],
> with longsuffering, for bearing one another in love;
> Endeavouring to keep the unity of the Spirit, even in
> the bond of peace; there is one body and one Spirit
> even as ye are called in one hope of your calling.
> (Ephesians 4:1–4)

Paul renewed this call in the epistle to the Colossian disciples.

> Put on therefore, as elect of God, holy and beloved
> [bowels] of mercies, kindness, humbleness of mind,
> meekness, longsuffering. (Colossians 3:12)

Jesus gave the charge equally to his disciples; he made it clear only
those who humbly obeyed his words and commands were his
disciples.

> Then said Jesus to those Jews which believed on him;
> if ye continue in my word, then are ye my disciples
> indeed. (John 8:31)

> Let this mind be in you, which was also in Christ
> Jesus: Who, being in the form of God, thought it
> not robbery to be equal with God: But made himself
> of no reputation, and took upon him the form of a
> servant, and was made in the likeness of men. And
> being found in fashion as a man, he humbled himself,
> and became obedient unto death, even the death of
> the cross. Wherefore God also hath highly exalted
> him, and given him a name which is above every
> name. (Philippians 2:5–9)

4. Truthfulness

Disciples must speak and demonstrate the truth at all times; this truth
they know and apply will set their converts free from the enemy.
They must not fall short of speaking and emphasizing this at all times.

True disciples of Christ must always be willing to walk in the divine truths of God. This is because divine truth will set their converts free of the world of sin and evil. This truth, however, comes from the revelation of God's Word, the Bible.

> Lie not one to another, seeing that ye have put off the
> old man with his deeds. (Colossians 3:9)

5. Passion for Lost Souls

Disciples must always have a burning zeal for lost souls. They must be winner of lost souls and publishers of the good news.

> The Lord gave the word: great was the company of
> those that published it. (Psalm 68:11)

> Go ye therefore, and teach all nations, baptising them
> in the name of the Father, and of the Son, and of
> the Holy Ghost; teaching them to observe all things
> whatsoever I have commanded you; and lo, I am with
> you always, even unto the end of the world, Amen.
> (Matthew 28:19–20)

6. Lights to the World

Disciples are lights to the world of darkness and spiritual guides for the blind. They must be torchbearers to the world. Their light must be enveloping to reach the inner recesses of the darkness of this wicked world.

Ye are the light of the world. A city that is set on an hill cannot be hid; neither do men light a candle and put it under a bushel, but on a candle stick; and it is giveth light unto all that are in the house: let your light so shine before men, that they may see your good works, and glorify your father which is in Heaven. (Matthew 5:14–16)

The apostle Paul put this fact in this light.

And art confident that thou thyself art a guide of the blind, a light of them which are in darkness. (Romans 2:19)

7. Joyful

Disciples must be joyful and therefore sources of joy for others. The joy of the Lord they manifest is their strength for doing the Lord's work. The prophet Isaiah wrote,

Therefore with joy shall ye draw water out of the wells of salvation. (Isaiah 12:3)

The water here represents the life-giving presence of the Holy Spirit. Discipleship is not attained through human efforts but through the power of the Spirit.

Ye are the salt of the earth [the joy of the earth]. (Matthew 5:3)

8. Anointed by the Power of God

Disciples must command and demonstrate the divine power of God. They must exercise dominion and authority over the world of darkness, being partakers of the divine nature.

> For whatsoever is born of God, overcometh the world; for this is the victory that overcometh, even our faith. (1 John 5:4)

9. Holy

Disciples must be holy, pure, and chaste. They must be separated and sanctified to please God, who has called them to discipleship.

> If ye were of the world, the world would love his own but because ye are not of the world, but I have chosen you out of the world, therefore the world hateth you. (John 15:19)

This holiness must be comprehensively built and sustained. It must involve both the external and internal aspects of the Christian believer for it to be acceptable to the Lord (Matthew 23:25–26). It calls for total separation from sin in its many forms. Paul reminded his spiritual son, Timothy, of this fact.

> No man that warreth [disciples] entangleth himself with the affairs of this life, that he may please him who hath chosen him to be a soldier. (2 Timothy 2:4)

It is holiness unto God that consecrates a disciple unto the Lord.

> Follow peace with all men and holiness without which no man shall see the Lord. (Hebrews 12:14)

The apostle Peter captured this revelation in this light.

> As obedient children, not fashioning yourselves according to the former lusts in your ignorance: But as he which hath called you is holy, so be ye holy in all manner of conversation; Because it is written, Be ye holy; for I am holy. But with the precious blood of Christ, as of a lamb without blemish and without spot: Who verily was foreordained before the foundation of the world, but was manifest in these last times for you, Who by him do believe in God, that raised him up from the dead, and gave him glory; that your faith and hope might be in God. Seeing ye have purified your souls in obeying the truth through the Spirit unto unfeigned love of the brethren, see that ye love one another with a pure heart fervently: Being born again, not of corruptible seed, but of incorruptible, by the word of God, which liveth and abideth for ever. (1 Peter 1:14–16, 19–23)

10. Loving

Disciples must be loving, admirable, amiable, and ready to manifest divine love and compassion. The hallmark of discipleship is an abiding divine love they share; this love is the bond of perfection that binds discipled brethren of the faith. It is the life and strength of discipleship.

> And above all these things put on charity, which is the bond of perfectness. (Colossians 3:14)

Jesus commanded the disciples to embrace this cornerstone virtue of love so it would make them stand out as his disciples.

> A new commandment I give unto you. That ye love one another as I have loved you, that ye also love one another. By this shall all men know that ye are my disciples, if ye have love for one another. (John 13:34, 35)

Peter asked us to continue in love one to another so the kingdom of God would be expanded beyond measure.

> Above everything, love one another earnestly, because love covers over many sins. (1 Peter 4:8)

11. Faithful

Disciples must have an abiding, living faith; they must be capable of trusting and relying on the God of their salvation. It is impossible to please God without faithfulness to his commands and instructions. This faith must be a living and positive one to have any useful impact on heavenly discipleship programs.

> Let not your heart be troubled; ye believe in God,
> believe also in me. (John 14:1–6)

> For without faith it is impossible to please Him, for
> he comes to God must believe that He is a rewarder
> of those who diligently seek Him. (Hebrews 11:6)

Faith is a pivotal hallmark of true Christian discipleship, and God expects his church on earth to regularly walk in the realm of abiding, living faith. Discipleship without faith or absolute trust in God is like a car without fuel. The greater the degree of faith a disciple develops and maintains, the more fruitful is the discipleship generated in the church community. This no doubt earns our divine approval and sets a divine seal on our discipleship work for the Lord.

Faith is the spiritual seal that cements the divine contract that exits between God, who is the owner of discipleship, and the Christian believer. Without faith, therefore, this spiritual contract would not be binding or effective.

12. Consecrated—Committed and Submissive

Disciples must be committed and loyal; they must keep this uppermost in their hearts. True disciples of Christ must be willing, more than anything else, to submit to their Master for training and empowerment. This will enable them to receive useful instruction and divine directions for true discipleship.

> So likewise, whosoever he be of you that forsaketh
> not all he hath, he cannot be my disciple. (Luke 14:33)

Disciples cannot be effective unless they surrender to the leading, the instructions, and the directions of Jesus Christ. The apostle Paul understood this revealed truth when he wrote in Philippians 4 that he could do all things relying on the grace of God. He said he was totally crucified to world and completely dedicated to his Master, Jesus Christ. This no doubt helped him finish his fruitful discipleship work he rendered to God. This was because he had totally submitted to the leading and instructions of God. Jesus made this point clearer when he told us in John 15 that unless we consecrated ourselves to his leading and instructions, we could not be effective in bearing the fruit of Christian discipleship.

13. Christlike

Disciples must be like their Master and ready to look up to him continually to receive instructions, wisdom, and knowledge to accomplish the task of discipleship committed into their hands. They must strictly follow Jesus' doctrines and continue his work.

> The disciple is not above his master; but every one that is perfect shall be as his master. (Luke 6:40)

> Then said Jesus to those Jews which believe on him, if ye continue in my word, then are ye my disciples indeed. (John 8:31)

> Behold, what manner of love the Father hath bestowed upon us, that we should be called the sons of God: therefore the world knoweth us not, because it knew him not. Beloved, now are we the sons of God, and

it doth not yet appear what we shall be: but we know that, when he shall appear, we shall be like him; for we shall see him as he is. And every man that hath this hope in him purifieth himself, even as he is pure. (1 John 3:1–3)

Christ uses his disciples to send the message of true salvation to a lost and directionless world enveloped in gross darkness. His disciples must therefore be willing, more than ever, to take on the characteristics of their Master to adequately represent him.

Friends, being like Christ is a true mark of effective discipleship, and God expects his redeemed disciples to put on the image and nature of Jesus in the course of bearing the fruits of discipleship.

14. Efficient Fruit Bearers

Finally, good disciples must be efficient fruit bearers; they must win and disciple lost souls into the kingdom of God.

> Ye have not chosen me, but I have chosen you, and ordained you, that ye should go and bring forth fruit and that your fruit should remain. (John 15:9)

To achieve this goal, disciples must always pray, fast, and be watchful.

> Let your loins be girded about and your lights burning: Be ye therefore ready also; for the son of man cometh at an hour when ye think not. (Luke 12:35, 40)

In Luke 18, Jesus advised his disciples to pull through their discipleship with fervent, persistent prayers.

> And He spoke a parable unto them to this end, that men ought always to pray and not faint. (Luke 18:1)

CHAPTER 3

Who Makes a Disciple?

Follow me and I will make you fishers of men.
—Matthew 4:19

I raised up some of your sons as prophets, and
some of your young men as Nazarites. Is it not
so, O ye children of Israel? says the LORD.
—Amos 2:11

Disciples are made by the Lord and given special, divine abilities
to accomplish the assignments of discipleship committed into their
hands. God calls, ordains, and commissions disciples with specific
messages to be passed on to others for the expansion of his kingdom
on earth. Jesus made this point clear.

Ye have not chosen me, but I have chosen you, and
ordained you that ye should go and bring forth fruit,
and that your fruit should remain. (John 15:9)

The apostle Paul presented this revelation in this light.

> And how shall they preach except they be sent? As
> it is written, how beautiful are the feet of them that
> preach the Gospel of peace and bring glad tidings of
> good things. (Romans 10:15)

Discipleship is a very crucial and all-encompassing divine
assignment that demands special power or supernatural enablement
for accomplishment. No one ever calls himself or herself into this
program and succeeds.

> And no man taketh this honour unto himself, but he
> that is called of God, as was Aaron. (Hebrews 5:4)

God is the only source of true discipleship. He has all the know-how
required for a successful discipleship program. God has called every
believer through the divine act of the salvation of Calvary to be a
good soldier of his kingdom. The believer has been redeemed to
serve God in one category of discipleship or the other.

> No man that warreth entangleth himself with the
> affairs of this life: that he may please Him who hath
> chosen him to be a soldier. (2 Timothy 2:4)

The prophet Jeremiah broadened this revelation.

> Then the word of the Lord came unto me, saying:
> before I formed thee in the belly I knew thee; and
> before thou comest forth out of the womb I sanctified
> thee and ordained thee a prophet unto the nations.
> (Jeremiah 1:4, 5)

Friends in the Lord, it is very dangerous to assume that disciples are made through human capabilities. I read a book on discipleship by an American Christian author who wrote through his assuming limited human knowledge that disciples are made and not born. It is my avowed prayer that the good Lord Jesus opens the spiritual eyes of this minister to see the degree of irreparable damage such misrepresentation of divine information has caused many who read his book. Disciples are not made by limited human know-how but are divinely called, ordained, equipped, sanctified, and sent forth by the Lord. John the Baptist presented this revealed truth in this way.

> John answered and said, a man can receive nothing
> except it be given him from Heaven. (John 3:27)

The beloved apostle John put it thus.

> But the anointing which ye have received of him
> abideth in you, and ye need not that any man teach
> you. But as the same anointing teacheth you of all
> things and is truth and is no lie and even as it hath
> taught, ye shall abide in him. (1 John 2:27)

Friends, I believe strongly in this scriptural insight that leads to a fruitful discipleship. It is this power-giving presence of God that initiates, propels, motivates, and sustains discipleship. This gift comes from God, no one else. The anointing of God teaches and equips believers for successful, fruit-bearing discipleship. It makes disciples of men and women for the Lord.

> How God anointed Jesus of Nazareth with the Holy
> Ghost and with power: who went about doing good
> and healing all that were oppressed by the devil; for
> God was with Him. (Acts 10:38)

The apostle Paul, realizing that God was the one who called, equipped, and made him an apostolic and missionary disciple, went straight after the divine instructions he received from the Lord into Arabia for a preparatory missionary discipleship program.

> For I neither received it of man, neither was I taught
> it, but by the revelation of Jesus Christ; But when it
> pleased God who separated me from my mother's
> womb and called me by grace; to reveal his son in
> me that I might preach him among the heathen;
> immediately I conferred not with flesh and blood;
> neither went I up to Jerusalem to them which were
> apostles before me; but I went into Arabia, and
> returned again unto Damascus; Then after three years
> I went up to Jerusalem to see Peter, and abode with
> him fifteen days. (Galatians 1:12, 15, 18)

No one but the Lord ever calls or trains anyone to be a fruit-bearing disciple. The best a believer can do, under the unction and leading of the Holy Spirit, is to assist in the training of disciples as perhaps advisors.

The great revelation behind this divine truth is that the power of discipleship is immediately conferred on believers as soon as they receive the salvation of the cross; God empowers them for discipleship or divine service as soon as they faithfully carry his cross daily and submit to his training and equipping.

> But as many as received him, to them gave he power
> to become the sons of God, even to them that believe
> on his name. (John 1:12)

In the discipleship program of the early church, the apostles and disciples looked strongly upon the Lord and received divine increase and unimaginable success. The Lord added as many disciples as he wished. The apostles and disciples never relied on their limited human knowledge and capabilities; rather, they depended on the prompting and leading of the Holy Spirit.

> And when they had prayed, the place was shaken
> where they were assembled together; and they were
> all filled with the Holy Ghost and they spoke the
> word of God with boldness. (Acts 2:31)
>
> Praising God and having favour with all the people:
> and the Lord added to the church daily such as should
> be saved. (Acts 2:47)

It is important to note that God had ordained and programmed the art of discipleship as part of his plan of salvation for mankind even before he created mankind. Therefore, any human effort of making disciples outside this general divine program of God will be totally fruitless.

> And we know that all things work together for good
> to them that love God, to them who are the called

according to his purpose; moreover whom he did
predestinates them he also called; and whom he called
them he also justified; and whom he justified, them
also he glorified. (Romans 8:28, 30)

Which purpose? The answer is simple! The purpose of fruit-bearing
discipleship. Friends, discipleship is a divine act that demands divine
wisdom and unction or supernatural power for accomplishment.
Otherwise, no positive effects result. It does not require the enticing
and the destructive wisdom of man. Paul exhorted the Corinthian
church concerning the aforementioned revealed truth.

And my speech and my preaching was not with
enticing words of man's wisdom, but in demonstration
of the spirit and of power; that your faith should not
stand in the wisdom of men but in the power of God.
(1 Corinthians 2:4, 5)

The wisdom of man, which is the wisdom of this wicked world
laden with destructive lusts and fashions, has no capability of making
fruit-bearing disciples because the ways of humanity are imperfect
before the Lord.

For my thoughts are not your thoughts, neither are
your ways my ways, saith the Lord. For as the heavens
are higher than the earth, so are my ways higher than
your ways, and my thoughts than your thoughts. For
as the rain cometh down, and the snow from heaven,
and returneth not thither, but watereth the earth, and
maketh it bring forth and bud, that it may give seed to

the sower, and bread to the eater: So shall my word be that goeth forth out of my mouth: it shall not return unto me void, but it shall accomplish that which I please, and it shall prosper in the thing whereto I sent it. (Isaiah 55:8–11)

There is a way which seemeth right unto a man, but the end thereof are the ways of death. (Proverbs 14:12)

This personal testimony of an orthodox minister contributing from his book *Really, Jesus Is Alive and Close* lends more credence and buttresses this point.

Though I had a very powerful orientation towards God during my [1] primary and secondary school days, but this apparently disappeared with my studies in philosophy: I became very sceptical in mentality and got so much taken by existentialism as a philosophical position; I had a wrong idea of the existentialist notion of self-determination which did not have much to do with God and prayers.

Men have polluted the doctrines and teachings of Jesus Christ and his Father. Subsequently, the doctrines, traditions and commandments of people have been used in human institutions as standards for the training of ne'er-do-well disciples of people and not of God. This orthodox minister wasted his years in a seminary and is not led or prompted by the Holy Spirit. He acquired useless, demonic

---

[1]   Kanayo P. Madu, Really Jesus is Alive and Close, Enugu,Ngeria,Snaap Press Limited,1995,P.26

philosophical and theological knowledge. No wonder the apostle Paul admonished the believers at the Corinthian church not to be given to this worldly wisdom.

> For the wisdom of this world is foolishness with God; for it is written, He taketh the wise in their own craftiness; and again, the Lord knoweth the thoughts of the wise that they are vain; therefore let no man glory in men; for all things are yours. (1 Corinthians 3:19–21)

Friends, if we must be truly relevant and fruitful in this end-time apostolic discipleship program of God, people like the orthodox minister above must be willing, as a matter of divine urgency, to forgo all irrelevant philosophical and theological human knowledge and submit to the training, equipping, and programming of the Holy Spirit. Every religious and doctrinal convention must be smashed and tossed into the dustbin of history. God must be given a free hand to make, equip, and commission disciples for effective fruit-bearing.

When we allow the Lord to make disciples for his Father's kingdom, a positive and glorious effect of discipleship becomes apparent. Better and stronger disciples are made and equipped for divine service. He fashioned Peter from a weak reed into a stone (Cephas). Upon this stone he anchored his discipleship program.

> And I say also unto thee, That thou art Peter, and upon this rock I will build my church; and the gates of hell shall not prevail against it. (Matthew 16:18)

> And he brought him to Jesus; and when Jesus behold him, he said, thou art Simon the son of Jona: Thou shalt be called Cephas, which is by interpretation a stone. (John 1:42)

Jesus commanded his disciples to forsake their fishing for fish for the discipleship program of fishing for men for the heavenly kingdom on earth. He trained, equipped, and made them effective fruit-bearing disciples who stood the test of time. Even as he ascended into heaven, he never left them without infilling them with power from above as was evident on the day of Pentecost.

> But ye shall receive power, after that the Holy Ghost is come upon you: and ye shall be witnesses unto me both in Jerusalem, and in all Judaea, and in Samaria, and unto the uttermost part of the earth. (Acts 1:8)

As you heed this discipleship call, have you left all and followed Jesus for infilling and training?

> And Jesus, walking by the sea of Galilee, saw two brethren, casting a net into the sea; for they were fishers; and he saith unto them, follow me and I will make you fishers of men: and they straightway left their nets and followed him. (Matthew 4:18–20)

Until the Lord makes and ordains His disciples for the end-time harvest, nothing practically possible will ever be attained by people alone. Unless the Lord builds the discipleship ark, all human effort will be wasted. The church will go only in circles.

> Except the Lord build the house, they labour in vain
> that build it; except the Lord keep the city, the watch
> man waketh but in vain. (Psalm 127:1)

In Acts, God made Cornelius a disciple and sent Peter to him as a point of contact to launch Cornelius into this divine service; this was physical ordination. It was not the apostle Peter who made him and others disciples but the Lord. God reserves the unquestionable right of making and ordaining disciples.

> He saw in a vision evidently about the ninth hour of
> the day an angel of God coming in to him, and saying
> unto him, Cornelius; and when he looked on him,
> he was afraid and said what is it Lord? And he said
> unto him, Thy prayers and thine alms come up for
> memorial before God. And now send man to Joppa
> and call for one Simon a tanner, whose house is by the
> seaside; he shall tell thee what thou oughtest-to-do.
> (Acts 10:3–6)

Our Lord Jesus broadened this revelation thus.

> All that the father giveth me [disciples] shall come to
> me, and him that cometh to me I will in no wise cast
> out; no man [disciple] can come to me, except the
> Father which sent me draw him; and I will raise him
> up at the last day. (John 6:37, 44)

I fervently pray the Lord will make fruitful disciples out of you for his end-time harvests in Jesus' name, amen.

CHAPTER 4

Rewarding Effects of Discipleship

And believers were the more added to the Lord,
multitudes both of men and women.
—Acts 5:4

Discipleship makes room for the expansion of the kingdom of God on earth and in heaven. It is our opportunity to tap into God's infinite resources. Many noticeable effects and rewards accompany God's discipleship program via the unction of the Holy Spirit. One of the greatest effects of discipleship is a divine increase in disciples, true believers.

After the Pentecost, discipleship assumed a pronounced dimension. The multiplication of the followers of Christ led to the expansion of God's kingdom on earth.

> And when the day of Pentecost was fully come, they were all with one accord in one place; and suddenly there came a sound from Heaven as of a rushing mighty wind, and it filled all the house where they were sitting; and they were all filled with the Holy

Ghost, and began to speak with other tongues, as the
Spirit gave them utterance. Then they that gladly
received his word were baptised; and the same day
there were added unto them about three thousand
souls. (Acts 2:1, 2, 4, 41)

Discipleship represents the unrestrained access to the divine increase
of God as well as a physical platform for enduring, uninterrupted
fellowship with God.

And they continued steadfastly in the apostles'
doctrine and fellowship, and in breaking of bread,
and in prayers; praising God and having favour with
all the people. And the Lord added to the church daily
such as should be saved. (Acts 2:47)

The divine plan of God for mankind from the beginning of ages has
been one of supernatural increase in every area of life. The mystery
behind divine increase is supernatural strength. This is why God
commanded the creatures to reproduce.

And God blessed them, and God said unto them
be fruitful and multiply and replenish the earth and
subdue it; and have dominion over the fish of the sea
and over the fowl of the air, and over every living
thing that moveth upon the earth. (Genesis 1:28)

This power or strength represents the Holy Spirit of God, which he
gives when discipleship is faithfully carried out.

> And I will pray the Father, and he shall give you another Comforter, that he may abide with you for ever; Even the Spirit of truth; whom the world cannot receive, because it seeth him not, neither knoweth him: but ye know him; for he dwelleth with you, and shall be in you. I will not leave you comfortless: I will come to you. (John 14:16–18)

The word *bless* means "empowered to prosper"; it represents the divine ability God gives us to increase in every area of life. True discipleship generates anointing (divine power) for exploits and accomplishments.

> Then he called his twelve disciples together, and gave them power and authority over all devils and to cure diseases. And he sent them to preach the kingdom of God, and to heal the sick. (Luke 9:1–2)

> And with great power gave the apostles witness of the resurrection of the Lord Jesus; and grace was upon them all. (Acts 4:33)

The word *grace* above means "divine power for accomplishment."

Salvation, Healing, and Deliverance

Committed, fruitful discipleship gives rise to genuine repentance that leads to salvation, healing, and deliverance of a lost world held under satanic bondage. It generates divine relief to the world. The spirit of discipleship has its divine target of setting captives free from all afflictions and works of darkness. The prophet Isaiah broadened this revelation in this perspective.

> The Spirit of the Lord God is upon me; because the Lord hath anointed me to preach good tidings unto the meek; he hath sent me to bind up the broken hearted, to proclaim liberty to the captives and the opening of the prison to them that are bound. To proclaim the acceptable year of the Lord and the day of vengeance of our God: to comfort all that mourn. (Isaiah 61:1)

The apostle Luke positioned this revelation thus.

> Then he called his twelve disciples together and gave them power and authority over all devils and to cure diseases; and he sent them to preach the Kingdom of God and to heal the sick. (Luke 9:1–2)

Jesus promised his disciples power that would aid them as disciples. It is of paramount importance that as long as the disciples continued in strict obedience to the Great Commission, increased power was continually released to them for this purpose.

> Behold, I give unto you power to tread on serpents and scorpions and over all the power of the enemy; and nothing shall by any means hurt you. (Luke 10:19)

The apostle Mark gave his own account.

And they went forth, and preached every where, the
Lord working with them and confirming the word
with signs following. Amen. (Mark 16:20)

A sign is an accompanying product of divine power that indicates
the lifting presence of the almighty God. This turning of the natural
into the supernatural results in physical manifestations. This power
for the replication of signs is obtainable through discipleship.

And by the hands of the apostles were many signs and
wonders wrought among the people; and they were
all with one accord in Solomon's porch. (Acts 5:12)

Discipleship produces salvation and deliverance from all the works
of Satan and his kingdom of darkness. It sets captives free and keeps
them comforted.

And he said unto them, go ye into all the world and
preach the Gospel to every creature; He that believeth
and baptised shall be saved; but he that believeth not
shall be damned. (Mark 16:15–16)

Insomuch that they brought forth the sick into the
streets, and laid them on beds and couches, that at the
least the shadow of Peter passing by might overshadow
some of them. There came also a multitude out of the
cities round about unto Jerusalem, bringing sick folks,
and them which were vexed with unclean spirits: and
they were healed every one. (Acts 5:15–16)

Jesus assured eternal salvation to many if he would be preached among the nations of the world. The hallmark of discipleship is the preaching of the good news of the kingdom of God to a lost world. This releases divine power for salvation and full restoration.

> And I, if I be lifted up from the earth, will draw all men unto me. (John 12:32)

The apostle Paul broadened this revelation.

> For I am not ashamed of the gospel of Christ: for it is the power of God unto salvation to every one that believeth; to the Jew first, and also to the Greek. (Romans 1:16)

> Whereof I was made a minister, according to the gift of the grace of God given unto me by the effectual working of his power. That he would grant you, according to the riches of his glory, to be strengthened with might by his Spirit in the inner man. (Ephesians 3:7, 16)

Increased Wisdom, Knowledge, and Revelation

Friends, discipleship represents the way to increased divine wisdom, knowledge, and revelation that are needed during this end time for the advancement of the work of the heavenly kingdom on earth. The end-time discipleship era is the apostolic age of divine wisdom and knowledge and revelation of mysteries. God has promised to release these for our discipleship programs.

> He answered and said unto them, because it is given unto you to know the mysteries of the Kingdom of heaven but to them it is not given; blessed are your eyes for they see; your ears for they hear. (Matthew 13:11, 16)

The apostle Luke presented it this way.

> For I will give you a mouth and wisdom, which all your adversaries shall not be able to gain say nor resist. (Luke 21:15)

Wisdom is the divine strategy the church requires earnestly for this kingdom work of discipleship, the Great Commission. Friends, God releases this end-time apostolic wisdom to enable us become efficient and fruitful disciples. As long as we faithfully heed this divine call, a corresponding level of wisdom, knowledge, and revelation will be released by God.

> If ye have heard of the dispensation of the grace of God which is given me to you-ward: How that by revelation he made known unto me the mystery; (as I wrote afore in few words, whereby, when ye read, ye may understand my knowledge in the mystery of Christ)Which in other ages was not made known unto the sons of men, as it is now revealed unto his holy apostles and prophets by the Spirit;

> And to make all men see what is the fellowship of the mystery, which from the beginning of the world hath been hid in God, who created all things by Jesus Christ: To the intent that now unto the principalities and powers in heavenly places might be known by the church the manifold wisdom of God. (Ephesians 3:2–5, 9–10)

Get set for a supernatural impartation of this divine wisdom.

In the course of his discipleship program, Stephen spoke with a level of divine wisdom that humbled and humiliated his detractors. They marveled at the beauty of the wisdom and knowledge God flowed through him.

> And they were not able to resist the wisdom and the Spirit by which he spoke. (Acts 6:11)

> Now when they saw the boldness of Peter and John, perceived that they were unlearned, and ignorant men, they marvelled; and they took knowledge of them, that they had been with Jesus; And beholding the man which was healed standing with them, they could say nothing against it. (Acts 4:13–14)

Prior to his ascension, Jesus promised the disciples the Spirit of the Father to help them spread the gospel and expand God's kingdom on earth. This Spirit of wisdom and revelation led to knowledge and understanding. Paul advised the disciples at Ephesus to ask from God this Spirit of wisdom and revelation to remain fruitful disciples and relevant in the discipleship programs of God.

Friends, without the Spirit of wisdom and revelation, no result will be achieved.

> That the God of our Lord Jesus Christ, the father of glory may give unto you the Spirit of wisdom and revelation in knowledge of Him: the eyes of your understanding being enlightened, that ye may know what is the hope of His calling, and what the riches of the glory of his inheritance in the saints. (Ephesians 1:17–18)

The gift of wisdom and revelation assisted the apostle Paul greatly in the course of his discipleship work for the Lord. This gift opened up a door for the brethren in Macedonia, and salvation came to many in that city.

> And a vision appeared to Paul in the night; There stood a man of Macedonia, and prayed him, saying, come over into Macedonia and help us; And after he had seen the vision, immediately we endeavoured to go unto Macedonia, assuredly gathering that the Lord had called us for to preach the gospel unto them: And from thence Philippi which is the chief city of that part of Macedonia, and colony: and we were in that city abiding certain days. (Acts 16:9–12)

Discipleship Generates Love and Divine Peace

Genuine discipleship ushers in an era of unity, love, peace, and prosperity in the church on earth. This situation makes room for an open heaven that will remove every lack and stop every retrogression.

> And the multitude of them that believed were of one heart and of one soul; neither said any of them that ought of the things which he possessed was his own; but they had all things common. (Acts 4:22)

The apostle John presented this revelation thus.

> By this shall all men know that ye are my disciples if ye have love one to another. (John 13:35)

Discipleship generates divine peace, which is the foundation of true discipleship. Jesus promised to leave his peace with the disciples to enable them to further the kingdom of God on earth. He was emphatic about this.

> Peace I leave with you, my peace I give unto you: not as the world giveth, give I unto you; let not your heart be troubled, neither let it be afraid. (John 14:27)

Love and peace truly represent some of the rewarding effects of fruitful discipleship.

Eternal Life

Eternal life is another important and most-rewarding effect of true discipleship. It assures one of living a blissful life in God's heavenly kingdom. God instituted the discipleship program to save as many as possible. The way to eternal life is through the gospel of Jesus Christ, the rallying point of the discipleship programs of the Lord.

> Jesus answered, "I am the way and the truth and the life. No one comes to the Father except through me." (John 14:6)

The apostle Paul put it this way.

> But now that you have been set free from sin and have become slaves of God, the benefit you reap leads to holiness, and the result is eternal life. For the wages of sin is death, but the gift of God is eternal life in Christ Jesus our Lord. (Romans 6:22–23)

The apostle John elucidated it further.

> Whoever believes in the Son has eternal life, but whoever rejects the Son will not see life, for God's wrath remains on them. (John 3:36)

Paul advised Timothy,

> But is now made manifest by the appearing of our saviour Jesus Christ, who hath abolished death and

hath brought life and immortality to light through the gospel. (2 Timothy 1:10)

For I am not ashamed of the gospel, because it is the power of God that brings salvation to everyone who believes: first to the Jews, then to the Gentiles. (Romans 1:16)

It is of paramount importance that the committed discipleship programs of the disciples of old brought salvation and eternal life to many lost, unsaved souls. A greater challenge is before us this era—to use the discipleship end-time programs of God to disciple souls originally headed for hell into everlasting life in heaven. The Lord is building an end-time apostolic ark of salvation that will carry the saved saints into heaven for eternity. I fervently pray God will make you part of this divine move in Jesus' mighty name, amen.

CHAPTER 5

The Role of the Holy Spirit in Discipleship

But ye shall receive power, after that the Holy Ghost is come upon you: and ye shall be witnesses unto me both in Jerusalem, and in all Judaea, and in Samaria, and unto the uttermost part of the earth.
—Acts 1:8

The Holy Spirit, the "doing" arm of the Trinity, executes the divine will and programs of God on earth. God in God, as I prefer to call the Holy Spirit, is the only being mandated by God the Father to carry out his discipleship work on earth. He is the expression of God's image, intents, and purposes that empower the sanctified children of God to discipleship. Without the Holy Spirit, our work for the Lord would be in vain and attract no reward.

> Except the Lord build the house, they labour in vain that build it: except the Lord keep the city, the watchman waketh but in vain. It is vain for you to rise up early, to sit up late, to eat the bread of sorrows: for so he giveth his beloved sleep. (Psalm 127:1–2)

The apostle John broadened this revelation.

> Abide in me, and I in you. As the branch cannot bear fruit of itself, except it abide in the vine; no more can ye, except ye abide in me. I am the vine, ye are the branches: He that abideth in me, and I in him, the same bringeth forth much fruit: for without me ye can do nothing. (John 15:4–5)

Hear Jesus as he condemned those disciples who embarked on discipleship programs on earth without the leadership of the Holy Spirit and his divine seal of approval.

> Not every one that saith unto me, Lord, Lord, shall enter into the kingdom of heaven; but he that doeth the will of my Father which is in heaven. Many will say to me in that day, Lord, Lord, have we not prophesied in thy name? and in thy name have cast out devils? and in thy name done many wonderful works? And then will I profess unto them, I never knew you: depart from me, ye that work iniquity. (Matthew 7:21–23)

Friends, discipleship is about fruit bearing, and only the divine energy or power of the Holy Spirit through absolute faith and obedience to Jesus will make this feasible.

Jesus promised us the gift of his Father, the Holy Spirit, before he ascended into heaven to assist us in carrying out the discipleship work he started and committed into our hands. Unfortunately, so many disciples of our time have fashioned their own discipleship programs that have produced little or no quality results. Friends, until we allow the Holy Spirit to play this paramount leadership role in the church unhindered, the Great Commission will continue to suffer setbacks, and the body of Christ the world over will continue to stink and depreciate in spiritual and physical values.

> The harvest is past, the summer is ended, and we are not saved. (Jeremiah 8:20)

> And I will pray the Father, and he shall give you another Comforter, that he may abide with you for ever; Even the Spirit of truth; whom the world cannot receive, because it seeth him not, neither knoweth him: but ye know him; for he dwelleth with you, and shall be in you. But the Comforter, which is the Holy Ghost, whom the Father will send in my name, he shall teach you all things, and bring all things to your remembrance, whatsoever I have said unto you. (John 14:16–17, 26)

The Holy Spirit must dwell in us to empower us and teach us the pathway to excellence and breakthrough in our discipleship. The gentle, empowering, and overcoming Spirit is waiting for us to be willing to be sanctified by him and available for faithful service before he can enter us for supernatural indwelling. It is this supernatural indwelling and incubation that attempts to start, sustain, and accomplish this discipleship work that will qualify us to gain God's divine approval and commendations. The apostle John extended this revelation.

> But ye have an unction from the Holy One, and ye
> know all things. But the anointing which ye have
> received of him abideth in you, and ye need not
> that any man teach you: but as the same anointing
> teacheth you of all things, and is truth, and is no lie,
> and even as it hath taught you, ye shall abide in him.
> (1 John 2:20, 27)

In Matthew 28, Jesus commissioned his disciples to go into the world and make disciples of men, as many as would believe the good news of the kingdom through uncompromising faith in him. He assured them of his divine presence, the Holy Spirit.

> Go ye therefore, and teach all nations, baptizing them
> in the name of the Father, and of the Son, and of the
> Holy Ghost: Teaching them to observe all things
> whatsoever I have commanded you: and, lo, I am
> with you always, even unto the end of the world.
> Amen. (Matthew 26:19–20)

Jesus understood the human limitations of his disciples to embark on this discipleship work. He knew it was not in their power to make things perfect, hence the need for the Holy Spirit to help execute and perfect the kingdom work.

> O LORD, I know that the way of man is not in
> himself: it is not in man that walketh to direct his
> steps. O LORD, correct me, but with judgment; not in
> thine anger, lest thou bring me to nothing. (Jeremiah
> 10:23–24)

Friends, the Holy Spirit is the divine seal God uses to accomplish the discipleship he has committed into our hands. He is the pathfinder who initiates, guides, and leads us into fruitful and radical breakthroughs in this ministry.

> And grieve not the Holy Spirit of God, whereby ye are sealed unto the day of redemption. (Ephesians 4:30)

When the Holy Spirit came upon Jesus in a dove-like form during his baptism in the River Jordan to confirm his earthly ministry, a carpenter became someone who attracted crowds. He rose from the lowly position of the ordinary to the extraordinary. Jesus, in the strength of the Spirit's empowering, made multitudes of disciples.

> And it came to pass in those days, that Jesus came from Nazareth of Galilee, and was baptized of John in Jordan. And straightway coming up out of the water, he saw the heavens opened, and the Spirit like a dove descending upon him: And there came a voice from heaven, saying, Thou art my beloved Son, in whom I am well pleased. And immediately the spirit driveth him into the wilderness. Now as he walked by the sea of Galilee, he saw Simon and Andrew his brother casting a net into the sea: for they were fishers. And Jesus said unto them, Come ye after me, and I will make you to become fishers of men. And straightway they forsook their nets, and followed him. (Mark 1:9–12, 16–18)

And again he entered into Capernaum after some days; and it was noised that he was in the house. And straightway many were gathered together, insomuch that there was no room to receive them, no, not so much as about the door: and he preached the word unto them. (Mark 2:1–2)

Friends, we need the leadership role of the Holy Spirit urgently in the church because it has fallen to a reproachable level of sustained decay and decline spiritually and physically. The Holy Spirit was the pathfinder who commissioned and sustained the excellent and unquestionable breakthroughs in Jesus' earthly ministry. He said in the book of John that he was not alone on earth and that he could do nothing except by the power of his heavenly Father, the Holy Spirit.

But Jesus answered them, My Father worketh hitherto, and I work. Then answered Jesus and said unto them, Verily, verily, I say unto you, The Son can do nothing of himself, but what he seeth the Father do: for what things soever he doeth, these also doeth the Son likewise. For as the Father hath life in himself; so hath he given to the Son to have life in himself; And hath given him authority to execute judgment also, because he is the Son of man. (John 5:17, 18, 26–27)

The apostle Luke broadened this revelation.

How God anointed Jesus of Nazareth with the Holy Ghost and with power: who went about doing good, and healing all that were oppressed of the devil; for God was with him. (Acts 10:38)

Hear Jesus himself confirming this revealed truth.

> And they called them, and commanded them not to
> speak at all nor teach in the name of Jesus. But Peter
> and John answered and said unto them, Whether it be
> right in the sight of God to hearken unto you more
> than unto God, judge ye. (Acts 4:18–19)

Friends in the Lord, the Holy Spirit assisted Jesus greatly in his
discipleship program. This Spirit power of God made him
extraordinary. He expounded the Scriptures and preached this gospel
of the kingdom with marvelous and unprecedented fervor that led
to breakthroughs and accomplishments that marveled and silenced
the religious leaders and critics of his ministry. This development
consequently enabled him to make multitudes of followers and
disciples.

> And they were all amazed, insomuch that they
> questioned among themselves, saying, What thing is
> this? What new doctrine is this? For with authority
> commandeth he even the unclean spirits, and they do
> obey him. (Mark 1:27)

The Holy Spirit assisted the evangelist Philip in his discipleship work
and led him to convert the Ethiopian eunuch, who incidentally
brought salvation to Africa.

It is in the power of the Holy Spirit, who has foreknowledge of all
things, to assist us in breaking through unreached frontiers and lands
that needs to be discipled for the Lord. Truly speaking, the evangelist

Philip was being assisted and empowered in an evangelistic crusade meeting in the city of Samaria when suddenly the Spirit of God led him to go down the lonely deserts of Gaza to harvest a disciple into the kingdom of God, the first African convert to the kingdom.

> Therefore they that were scattered abroad went every where preaching the word. Then Philip went down to the city of Samaria, and preached Christ unto them. And the angel of the Lord spake unto Philip, saying, Arise, and go toward the south unto the way that goeth down from Jerusalem unto Gaza, which is desert. And he arose and went: and, behold, a man of Ethiopia, an eunuch of great authority under Candace queen of the Ethiopians, who had the charge of all her treasure, and had come to Jerusalem for to worship. (Acts 8:4–5, 26–27)

Brethren, we can imagine and quantify the quality of discipleship that could be attained if we would humble ourselves as did Philip under the leadership of the Holy Spirit. Struggles, unfruitfulness, and confusion will be averted, and more souls will be won and converted to God. It is the empowering presence of God's Spirit that convicts and converts believers into the kingdom of God. Divine joy, direction, revelation, and qualitative increase precede spirit-led discipleship.

> And when they were come up out of the water, the Spirit of the Lord caught away Philip, that the eunuch saw him no more: and he went on his way rejoicing. (Acts 8:39; see also Acts 13:42–44, 48–49)

The Holy Spirit is a pathfinder who breaks through barriers and blazes the discipleship trail. He knows the unbroken and unreached grounds that needs tilling for planting and harvesting. The disciples of old relied mightily on the Holy Spirit during the harvest period of their era and recorded qualitative and unassailable volumes of success in their discipleship. It is of paramount importance to stress here that if we are to record greater work in the end-time harvest of the kingdom of God, which is very much at hand, we must as a matter of urgency relinquish all to the Holy Spirit to lead, guide, plan, and execute the work of the Great Commission. If we are obedient to him, we will remain eternally glad. Philip knew the promise of the Father, the Holy Spirit, and his function in the church of God, and he quickly yielded to him, and that made him record quality success in his evangelistic ministry.

> Then the Spirit said unto Philip, Go near, and join thyself to this chariot. And when they were come up out of the water, the Spirit of the Lord caught away Philip, that the eunuch saw him no more: and he went on his way rejoicing. But Philip was found at Azotus: and passing through he preached in all the cities, till he came to Caesarea. (Acts 8:29, 39–40)

The Holy Spirit separated Paul and Barnabas for discipleship. God, the owner of the work, knows through his Holy Spirit that those vessels were specially made and ordained for discipleship. He mandated his Spirit to execute this divine task.

> As they ministered to the Lord, and fasted, the Holy Ghost said, Separate me Barnabas and Saul for the

work whereunto I have called them. And when they had fasted and prayed, and laid their hands on them, they sent them away. So they, being sent forth by the Holy Ghost, departed unto Seleucia; and from thence they sailed to Cyprus. (Acts 13:2–4)

When the Holy Spirit is given the chance to operate through us and consequently takes hold of our discipleship program, he indwells us to perform miraculous works that draw people into God's kingdom. The world will not come to God's kingdom except when they see true signs and wonders made manifest. This obviously brings multitudes of believing disciples into the kingdom. He will enable us to identify error and falsehoods that oppose the truth of the gospel and deal squarely with them.

But Elymas the sorcerer (for so is his name by interpretation) withstood them, seeking to turn away the deputy from the faith. Then Saul, (who also is called Paul,) filled with the Holy Ghost, set his eyes on him. And said, O full of all subtlety and all mischief, thou child of the devil, thou enemy of all righteousness, wilt thou not cease to pervert the right ways of the Lord? And now, behold, the hand of the Lord is upon thee, and thou shalt be blind, not seeing the sun for a season. And immediately there fell on him a mist and a darkness; and he went about seeking some to lead him by the hand. Then the deputy, when he saw what was done, believed, being astonished at the doctrine of the Lord. And the next sabbath day came almost the whole city together to hear the word of God. But when the Jews saw the multitudes, they were filled with envy, and spake against those things which were spoken by Paul, contradicting and blaspheming. And when the Gentiles heard this, they were glad, and glorified the word of the Lord: and as many as were ordained to eternal life believed. (Acts 13:8–12, 44–45, 48)

A spirit-led discipleship program offers divine protection and support. God, through his spirit of revelation, gave the apostle Paul divine backing and assurance of protection in his ministry in Corinth. Luke wrote,

Then spake the Lord to Paul in the night by a vision, Be not afraid, but speak, and hold not thy peace: For I am with thee, and no man shall set on thee to hurt thee: for I have much people in this city. (Acts 18:9–10)

Brethren, God still has more people in cities and rural areas who must be reached. Let us yield to the gentle prompting of the Holy Spirit, who will enable us to break into these unreached lands, difficult terrain and hindrances notwithstanding. The apostle Paul basked in the euphoria of the zeal of the anointing of God in his life and left without the leading of the Spirit into Arabia for an unsuccessful missionary journey. He toiled without much result and came back after much frustration and unfruitfulness until the Holy Spirit separated him and Barnabas for successful discipleship. The same, sweet, gentle Holy Spirit led Paul, while at Troas, for successful work in Macedonia when he was at a crossroads as to where to continue. He was led through the Spirit of revelation to receive the Macedonian call for discipleship. Paul never hesitated to go to Macedonia for successful ministry.

> Now when they had gone throughout Phrygia and the region of Galatia, and were forbidden of the Holy Ghost to preach the word in Asia, After they were come to Mysia, they assayed to go into Bithynia: but the Spirit suffered them not. And a vision appeared to Paul in the night; There stood a man of Macedonia, and prayed him, saying, Come over into Macedonia, and help us. And after he had seen the vision, immediately we endeavoured to go into Macedonia, assuredly gathering that the Lord had called us for to preach the gospel unto them. (Acts 16:6–7, 9–10)

Brethren, the church is cold and unfruitful because we lack the Holy Spirit in full measure. If we could only allow him space through a deliberate act of deep consecration, he would bring into our churches souls by the hundreds and thousands as well as by ones and twos. He would sharpen and give us unassailable breakthroughs in our discipleship programs.

Hear Charles. H. Spurgeon throwing more revelational insights on this matter-of-fact truth.

> If we had the spirit sealing our ministry with power,
> it will signify very [2] little about talent. Men might be

---

[2]   Oswald J. Smith, The Revival we need, New York, The Christian Alliance Publishing Company, 1925, Chapter 4, page 1.

poor and uneducated, their words might be broken and ungrammatical, but if the mind of the spirit attended them, the humblest evangelist would be more successful than the most learned of divines, or the most eloquent preachers. It is extraordinary power from God, not talent, that wins the day. It is extraordinary spiritual unction, not extraordinary mental power that we need. Mental power may fill a chapel but spiritual power fills the church with soul anguish. Mental power may gather a large congregation, but only spiritual power will save souls. What we need is spiritual power.

Our beloved brother in the Lord, Arthur T. Pierson, sheds more divine insight on this revealed leadership role of the Holy Spirit in discipleship when he wrote under unction,

> Let the spirit be lacking, and there may be wisdom of words, but not the [3] wisdom of God; the powers of oratory, but not the power of God; the demonstration of argument and the logic of the schools, but not the demonstration of the Holy Spirit, the all-convincing logic of his lightening flash, such as convinced Saul before Damascus gate. When the spirit was outpoured the disciples were all filled with power from on high, the most unlettered tongue could silence gainsayers, and with its new fire burn its ways through obstacles as flames fanned by mighty winds sweep through forests.

---

[3]   Oswald J. Smith, The Revival we need, New York, The Christian Alliance Publishing Company, 1925; Chapter 4, page 1.

Brethren, I pray God will outpour his latter rain abundantly on you for the end-time harvest as he did in the old apostolic dispensation. Take this—it is highly prophetic: God has opened up his heaven for an outpouring of his end-time apostolic grace, the power of the Holy Spirit, anointing, for the end-time revival of the world. This apostolic anointing—the spiritual move of the Holy Spirit—is embedded in the wind he has sent forth.

> Who layeth the beams of his chambers in the waters: who maketh the clouds his chariot: who walketh upon the wings of the wind. (Psalm 104:3)

This was David the psalmist, prophesying under divine unction, the end-time outpouring of God's Spirit for fruitful discipleship.

It takes the spiritually anointed eyes of sanctified believers to discern this great spiritual outpouring. Brethren, each time God blows his wind, there is always revival and tremendous changes with accompanying blessings, breakthroughs, and open doors. This end-time spirit of revival is for the supernatural ordaining, calling, and commissioning of disciples for end-time harvest. After the descent of the Holy Spirit (Pentecost) in the old apostolic dispensation, more sanctified, fruitful apostles and disciples were made and commissioned by the Lord, and this led to tremendous discipleship. Brethren, the latter outpouring will far surpass the harvests of the first apostolic order.

> The glory of this latter house shall be greater than of the former, saith the LORD of hosts: and in this place will I give peace, saith the LORD of hosts. (Haggai 2:9)

Watch out for God's wonders this time. God is preparing more spirit-filled messengers like Charles Finneys, Smith Wigglesworths, and others of their like upon whom he will release the Holy Spirit's power for tremendous end-time harvests. Expect more of these spiritual giants from Africa, with special reference to Nigeria. Anyone who does not fit into this end-time outpouring of the spiritual power of God, the great Feast of Tabernacles, will be left behind, and heaven will forever remain closed to him or her.

> And it shall be, that whoso will not come up of all the families of the earth unto Jerusalem to worship the King, the Lord of hosts, even upon them shall be no rain. And if the family of Egypt go not up, and come not, that have no rain; there shall be the plague, wherewith the Lord will smite the heathen that come not up to keep the feast of tabernacles. This shall be the punishment of Egypt, and the punishment of all nations that come not up to keep the feast of tabernacles. (Zechariah 14:17–19)

Brethren, get set for this great Feast of Tabernacles, the spiritual outpouring that will herald the end-time revival that will shake the world; its impact will be felt in every home. It will open up graves in peoples' lives and bring every deadness to life. It will produce genuine repentance through conviction, confession, forsaking, remission of sins, and salvation. It will also carry in its wake the power of divine transformation and full restoration that will give birth to true love among believers in Christendom, divine supernatural increase, boldness, favor, wisdom, and a collection of divine revelations that will keep the machinery of the end-time discipleship programs of God permanently on course.

I plead with the churches of God, the true body of Christ the world over to close ranks in networking effectively for efficient and fruitful discipleship. We can all achieve this divine purpose if the Holy Spirit is allowed to take over the church of God for the initiation, planning, and execution of fruitful discipleship programs. Let us do away with the vain philosophies, the silly doctrines, and the wicked wisdom of humanity that have brought carnality and worldliness into the church of Christ. I exhort the churches to remove these hindrances from their structures and accept the leadership and progressive role of the Holy Spirit of God. God Bless.

CHAPTER 6

The Arts and Costs of Discipleship

For which of you, intending to build a tower, sitteth not down
first and counteth the cost whether he have sufficient to finish it?
—Luke 14:28

Discipleship involves the gathering and building up of people for the
eternal kingdom of God. It demands special provable methods that
entail many sacrifices. Discipleship is the highest level of responsibility
a person can undertake in life, and as a result, it requires special divine
methods and skills to attain the standard God expects. God initiated
this divine work of gathering and building his people preparatory
for entrance into his glorious kingdom to achieve a purpose. The
prophet Isaiah threw light on this revealed truth.

> The Lord God, which gathereth the outcasts of Israel,
> saith, yet will I gather others to him beside those that
> are gathered unto him. (Isaiah 56:8)

The arts and costs of discipleship imply the supernatural methods
and skills God imbues us with as well as the sacrifices we must make
for the construction of a successful discipleship program. This is so

important because God, our cobuilder, approves only works that have been tested in the furnace of the Holy Spirit. God demands us to build efficiently and faithfully.

> For we are labourers together with God: ye are God's husbandry, ye are God's building. According to the grace of God which is given unto me, as a wise masterbuilder, I have laid the foundation, and another buildeth thereon. But let every man take heed how he buildeth thereupon. Every man's work [discipleship] shall be made manifest: for the day shall declare it, because it shall be revealed by fire; and the fire shall try every man's work of what sort it is. If any man's work abide which he hath built thereupon, he shall receive a reward. (1 Corinthians 3:9–10, 13–14)

For this reason, the Lord has made the following proven methods available to assist us in building divinely approved works of discipleship.

Through the Ministry of the Word

> Go stand, and speak in the temple to the people all the words of this life: and daily in the temple, and in every house they cease not to teach and preach Jesus Christ. (Acts 5:20, 42)

Brethren, the first discernible art of discipleship is the ministry of the Word, which involves the teaching and preaching of the Word to a lost, decadent, and dying world. Jesus commenced his discipleship ministry with preaching and teaching the good news of the kingdom of God.

> Now after that John was cast into prison, Jesus came into Galilee, preaching the gospel of the kingdom of God: and saying, the time is fulfilled and the kingdom of God is at hand; repent and believe the gospel. (Mark 1:14–15)

> Now when Jesus had heard that John was cast into prison, he departed into Galilee; from that time Jesus began to preach and to say repent: for the kingdom of heaven is at hand; and Jesus walking by the sea of Galilee, saw two brethren, Simon called peter, and Andrew his brother, casting a net into the sea; for they were fishers. And he saith unto them, follow me and I will make you fishers of men; and they straight away left their nets and followed him. (Matthew 4:12, 17, 20)

Brethren, the Word of God carries a special anointing that restores and gives life to dying souls. Remember, discipleship involves gathering lost souls into the eternal kingdom of God. The Word of God locates, arrests, convicts, and sets sinners free from the pollutions and carnality of this world. This obviously leads to full divine restoration and in return draws disciples into God's kingdom. The kingdom of God is a prepared place of renewed divine life he wants us to bring disciples into; his word carries this divine life, and only by the true teaching and preaching of the Word can this drawing life be made manifest, and then shall multitudes of disciples be drawn to God's enduring kingdom. Jesus presented this revelation when he wrote,

> It is the spirit of God that quickeneth the flesh profiteth nothing; the words I speak unto you they are spirit; and they are life. (John 6:63)

That is to say the Spirit (*rhema* in Greek) in the Word of God draws people into the kingdom of God.

> In the beginning was the word, and the word was with God, and the word was God. In Him was life; and the life was the light of men. (John 1:1, 4)

> Search the scriptures; for in them ye think ye have eternal life: and they are they which testify of me. And ye will not come to me, that ye might have life. (John 5:39–40)

When God calls and ordains someone for discipleship, he equips and gives that person the Word to preach and teach the people. He doesn't send someone out without the Word to convict and draw disciples into his kingdom. Before prophet Jeremiah started his discipleship ministry, God sufficiently armed him with his Word. He prospered in the strength of this divine equipping.

> Before I formed thee in the belly I knew thee; and before thou camest forth out of the belly I knew thee; and ordained thee a prophet unto the nations; then the Lord put forth His hand and touched my mouth.

And the Lord said unto me, behold, I have put my words in your mouth. (Jeremiah 1:5, 9)

In the same way, the prophet Ezekiel was properly equipped and armed by God with his word of conviction and conversion in addition to the corresponding anointing to sufficiently carry out his discipleship program.

> And the spirit entered into me when he spake unto me and set me upon my feet, that I heard Him that spake unto me; and he said unto me, son of man, I send thee to the children of Israel, to a rebellious nation that hat rebelled against me; they and their fathers, have transgressed against me, even unto this very day; and thou shall speak my words unto them, whether they will hear or whether they will forebear; for they are most rebellious: but thou, son of man, hear what I say unto thee. Be not thou rebellious like that rebellious house; open thy mouth and eat that I give thee. And I looked, behold, a hand was sent unto me, and, lo, a roll of book was therein. (Ezekiel 2:2, 3, 7, 8, 9)

In 1996, approximately a year after the Lord called me into full-time ministry, he spoke to me through his word in Isaiah and gave me a specific message to deliver to disciples he draws through me.

> As for me, this is my covenant with them, saith the Lord; my spirit that is upon thee, and my words which I have put in thy mouth, shall not depart out of thy

mouth, nor out the mouth of thy seed, saith the Lord, from henceforth and for ever. (Isaiah 59:21)

Ever since that divine encounter, our ministry's discipleship program that was yielding few results improved tremendously.

The disciples and apostles of the old apostolic order drew multitudes of disciples into God's kingdom through the Word. They set villages, cities, countries, and regions aflame with the Word and the good news of the kingdom. Peter preached and taught the Word and brought three thousand people into the kingdom in his first successful sermon. It was so electrifying and captivating that the convicted souls asked for a way out of their bondage and accepted the renewed kingdom life that discipleship offers. They were as a result baptized into God's kingdom. These were people who previously mocked the disciples, who had just received the Pentecost outpouring for the work of the Great Commission.

But Peter, standing up with the eleven, lifted up his voice and said unto them, ye men of Judea, and all ye that dwell at Jerusalem, be this known unto you, and hearken to my words; therefore let all the house of Israel know assuredly, that God had made the same Jesus, whom, ye have crucified, both the Lord and Christ; now when they heard this, they were pricked in their hearts, and said unto peter and to the rest of the apostles, men and brethren, what shall we do?; then peter said unto them, repent and be baptised every one of you in the name of Jesus Christ for the remission of sins, and ye shall receive, the gift of the Holy Ghost; and with many other words did he testify and exhort saying, save yourselves from this untowered generation; then they that gladly received his word were baptised and the same day there were added unto them about three thousands souls. (Acts 2:14, 36–38, 40, 41)

This unique sermon by the apostle Peter coincidentally opened up the floodgate for widespread discipleship. The other disciples, excited with this divine move, scattered abroad and with the Word, set cities and regions ablaze, winning souls for the kingdom. They were so consumed with zeal that the ministry of the Word became their major preoccupation, and this expanded God's kingdom. They resisted diversion and distractions even when Satan created disputes over food to slow them down. The Devil saw tremendous numbers being discipled into the kingdom of God and purposed to cleverly checkmate the efforts of the disciples. I pray we will resolutely resist or stop all satanic onslaught targeted at our discipleship programs of the end time; we must brace up and take a cue from the disciples of the old apostolic order.

In those days, when the number of disciples was multiplied, there arose a murmuring of the Grecians against the Hebrews because their widows were neglected in daily ministration. Then the twelve called the multitudes of the disciples unto them, and said, it is not reason that we should leave the word of God, and serve tables. Wherefore brethren look ye out among you seven men of honest report, full of the Holy Ghost and wisdom, whom we may appoint over this business; but we will give ourselves continually to prayer and to the ministry of the word. And the word of God increased; and the number of the disciples multiplied in Jerusalem greatly; and a great company of the priests were obedient to the faith. (Acts 6:1–4, 7)

The preaching of the Word gave the evangelist Philip resounding success in his evangelistic ministry; numerous disciples were drawn into the kingdom through the deliberate art of preaching the Word.

Therefore they that were scattered abroad went everywhere preaching the word; then Philip went down to the city of Samaria, and preached Christ unto them. And the people with one accord gave heed unto those things which Philip spake, hearing and seeing the miracles which he did. But when they believed Philip preaching the things concerning the kingdom of God, and the name of Jesus Christ, they baptised both men and women. (Acts 8:4–6, 12)

The apostle Paul, the master builder and one of the most fruitful disciples of the Lord, employed the art of preaching and teaching the Word for the harvest of quality souls into the kingdom. He was a seasoned teacher of the Word, and with a special unction (power of the Holy Spirit), he brought wonderful revelations and divine insights that made his discipleship work exciting and fruitful. His teaching or instructional skills were so splendid and result-oriented that the head of the discipleship programs, the apostle Peter, acknowledged it and quickly offered a hand of fellowship. These teaching skills brought salvation to many and thus expanded the kingdom of God.

And account that the longsuffering of our Lord is salvation; even as our beloved brother Paul also according to the wisdom given unto him hath written unto you; as also in all his epistles, speaking in them of these things, in which are some things hard to be understood which they that are unlearned and unstable wrest, as they do also the other scriptures, unto their own destruction. (2 Peter 3:15–16)

Paul corroborated this.

Our gospel came not unto you in word only, but also in power and in the Holy Ghost, and in much assurance. (1 Thessalonians 1:4)

It is not expedient for me doubtless to glory. I will come to visions and revelations of the Lord. I knew a man in Christ above fourteen years ago, (whether in the body, I cannot tell; or whether out of the body, I cannot tell: God knoweth;) such an one caught up to the third heaven. And I knew such a man, (whether in the body, or out of the body, I cannot tell: God knoweth;) How that he was caught up into paradise, and heard unspeakable words, which it is not lawful for a man to utter. Of such an one will I glory: yet of myself I will not glory, but in mine infirmities. For though I would desire to glory, I shall not be a fool; for I will say the truth: but now I forbear, lest any man should think of me above that which he seeth me to be, or that he heareth of me. And lest I should be exalted above measure through the abundance of the revelations, there was given to me a thorn in the flesh, the messenger of Satan to buffet me, lest I should be exalted above measure. (2 Corinthians 12:1–7)

He faithfully used the power of the word to achieve God's purpose of drawing multitudes of disciples into his kingdom. This power performed great exploits; it nearly convinced King Agrippa to become a Christian disciple. It made occult men who for long had practiced magic acts burn their materials and became converted.

Whereupon king Agrippa, I was not disobedient unto the heavenly vision [discipleship]: king Agrippa, believest thou the prophets? I know that thou believest; then Agrippa said unto Paul, almost thou persuadest me to be a Christian. (Acts 26:19, 27–28)

And he went into the synagogue, and spake boldly for the space of three months, disputing and persuading the things concerning the kingdom of God; and many that believed came, and confessed, and shewed their deeds. Many of them also which used curious arts brought their books together and burned them before all men … so mightily grew the word of God and prevailed. (Acts 19:8, 18–19)

Then Paul stood up, and beckoning with his hand said, men of Israel, and ye that fear God give audience; and the next Sabbath day came almost the whole city together to hear the word of God. But when the Jews saw the multitudes, they were filled with envy, and spake against those things which were spoken by Paul, contradicting and blaspheming. (Acts 13:16, 44–45)

Brethren, with this multitude-drawing power of the Word that followed the earlier disciples, we are being challenged more than ever to embrace the Word of God and activate it through the art of studying, teaching, and preaching so the power of God can be released into our respective ministry works for better results. When we get a strong hold on the Word, the power for the end-time harvest will be readily available for the salvation of millions of lost souls into the kingdom of our God. The apostle Paul caught this revelation.

For I am not ashamed of the gospel of Christ; for it is the power of God unto salvation. (Romans 1:16)

Study to show thyself approved unto God, a work man that needeth not to be ashamed, rightly dividing the word of truth. (2 Timothy 2:15)

Through Prayer and Fasting

Prayer and fasting are very important instruments for effective discipleship that meets God's standard. Jesus started his ministry by a forty-day and forty-night prayer and fasting session and continued with them and ended his ministry with them. He never underplayed the unique role of these arts of discipleship.

> And when He had fasted forty days and forty nights,
> he was afterward an hungered. (Matthew 4:2)

> And it came to pass about eight days after these sayings,
> he took Peter and John and James, and went up into a
> mountain to pray; and as he prayed the fashion of his
> countenance was altered, and his raiment was white
> and glistering. (Luke 9:28–29)

Brethren, it is highly instructive to conclude that prayer and fasting give tremendous impetus to our discipleship work we render to the Lord. They are the powerhouses that generate divine currents for effective discipleship. This matter-of-fact-reason informs why our Lord Jesus Christ maintained regular prayer schedules. During the day, he was busy with his Father's work of teaching, preaching the Word, and healing, but he retreated at night, alone, to pray his way into heaven through prayer. He usually came out in the morning with renewed divine power for greater exploits.

> And it came to pass in those days, that he called unto
> him his disciples … and the whole multitude sought
> to touch him, for there went virtue out of him, and
> healed them all. (Luke 6:12–13, 19)

Jesus finished his discipleship ministry, which had been approved by his heavenly Father, because he continued in prayer and fasting. He told this secret to us by advising us to continue to be constant in prayer. He counseled us this way.

> And he spake a parable unto them to this end; that
> man ought always to pray and not to faint. (Luke 18:1)

The apostle Paul advised us in a similar vein, having tasted this key of prayer and fasting with success in his discipleship works.

> Continue in prayer, and watch in the same with
> thanksgiving; withal praying also for us, that God
> would open unto us a door of utterance [success in
> discipleship] to speak the mystery of Christ, for which
> I am also in bond. (Colossians 4:2–3)

He continued in Thessalonians,

> Pray without ceasing; quench not the spirit.
> (1 Thessalonians 5:17–19)

Brethren, if we want to experience a mighty revival and divine increase in the end-time discipleship program of God, we urgently need to call in the spirit of prayer to inflame in us an unquenchable passion for saving lost souls. We must not quench the fire of prayer. We need intercessory and agonizing prayer and fasting sessions that will give rise to the expected power of revival the church of God desperately needs. Cold, dead, and carnal churches—and we have them all over—must earnestly desire to be aflame, revived, and awakened from deep spiritual slumber. This will happen only when we employ the art of effective, fervent, and agonizing prayer and watching, or fasting. The divine call of heaven to the churches is to wake up from spiritual sleep and brace up to the challenges God's end-time apostolic discipleship poses to us. The trumpet call is gone out; let us wake up and work.

> Awake, awake, put on thy strength, o Zion; put on thy beautiful garments, o Jerusalem the Holy city: for henceforth there shall no more come into thee the uncircumcised and the unclean: shake thyself from the dust; arise and sit down, O Jerusalem; loose thyself from the bands of thy neck, O captive daughter of Zion. (Isaiah 52:1–2)

The early apostles and disciples made far-reaching breakthroughs when they employed this art of prayer and fasting handed down to us by Jesus. They were so committed in the ministry of prayer and fasting that villages, towns, cities, and regions were aflame with heart-felt revival, and this gave the early apostles and disciples tremendous breakthroughs in their ministry of discipleship. It enabled them to avoid distractions and derailment of their heavenly vision. Mighty miracles, healing, joy, and salvation became manifest.

> But we will give ourselves continually to prayer and the ministry of the word: And the word of God increased; and the number of the disciples multiplied in Jerusalem greatly; and a great company of the priests were obedient to the faith. (Acts 6:4, 7)

> And when they had prayed, the place was shaken where they were assembled together; and they were all filled with the Holy Ghost and they spake the word of God with boldness; And the multitude of

them that believed were of one heart and one soul. (Acts 4:31–32)

Brethren, the power of prayer and fasting brings down divine boldness, love, unity, and supernatural increase. The boldness in the Word drives Satan away and convicts and converts lost souls for discipling into the body of Christ.

> The people that do know their God shall be strong [bold] and do exploits. (Daniel 11:32)

Finally, prayer and fasting initiates, increases, and sustains the discipleship works given to us by the Lord. Wake up, watch, pray, and remain successful disciples of the Lord. Apply the key of prayer and fasting Jesus has released to us. He has given us the keys of the kingdom to conduct fruitful and efficient discipleship. Prayer and fasting are some of these keys we should use to glorify God.

> And I will give unto thee the keys of the kingdom of heaven; and whatsoever thou shalt bind on earth shall be bound in heaven; and whatsoever thou shalt loose on earth, shall be loosed in heaven. (Matthew 16:19)

Evangelism: Soul Winning

> The Lord is not slack concerning his promise as some men count slackness; But is longsuffering to us-ward, not willing that any should perish, but that all should come to repentance. (2 Peter 3:9)

Evangelism, soul winning, is the hallmark of the discipleship program of God on earth. It is the heartbeat of God, and that is the major foundation on which the discipleship work of God rests. God perfected this art of soul winning with the historic and prophetic birth and death of Jesus.

> And as Moses lifted up the serpent in the wilderness, even so must the son of man be lifted up: That whosoever believeth in him should not perish, but have eternal life: for God so loved the world, that He gave His only begotten son, that whosoever believeth in Him should not perish, but have everlasting life. For God sent not His son into the world to condemn the world; but that the world through him might be saved. (John 3:14–17)

The prophet Isaiah broadened this revelation.

> For unto us a child is born, unto us a son is given: and the government shall be called upon his shoulder: and his name shall be called wonderful, counsellor, the mighty God, the everlasting father, the prince of peace; of the increase of His government and peace there shall be no end, upon the throne of David, and upon his kingdom, to order it, and to establish it with judgment and with justice from henceforth even forever. The zeal of the Lord of hosts will perform this: The Lord sent a word into Jacob, and it hath lighted upon Israel. (Isaiah 9:6–8)

The phrase "of the increase of his government and peace there shall be no end" above represents the perfected discipleship art of soul winning that God the master planner had earmarked to draw, save, and consequently restore enduring peace to a lost and hopeless world. Our merciful God loves lost sinners and wants them to forsake their evil ways and return to him.

> Behold I will send for many fishers, saith the Lord, and they shall fish them, and after will I send for many hunters, and they shall hunt them from every mountain, and from every hill and out of the holes of the rocks: for mine eyes are upon all their ways; they are not hid from my face, neither is their iniquity hid from my eyes. (Jeremiah 16:16–17)

The fishers and the hunters referred to above imply the divinely anointed and commissioned laborers or messengers God appointed to win lost souls for the kingdom. Once, Peter wanted to fish with his own wisdom and methods, but he had his plan changed by Jesus, who told Peter he wanted to make him a fisher of men, a discipler of men and women for the heavenly kingdom.

> And he saith unto them, follow me, and I will make you fishers of men; And they straightaway left their nets and followed him. (Matthew 4:19–20)

This paid off tremendously. Peter, through the divine art of soul-wining, became the physical anchor on which God rested his prophetic discipleship work on earth. In his first sermon at Jerusalem, which incidentally became the first evangelistic meeting ever, God through Peter saved and discipled over three thousands souls into his kingdom. This obviously became the trigger point by which the church's discipleship program assumed a resourceful dimension. The disciples scattered with an unquenchable zeal to accomplish the Great Commission. Philip caught this fire of evangelism and sailed to Samaria, following the scattering of the disciples in the wake of persecutions, and employed the art of soul-winning to harvest numerous souls for the kingdom.

> Therefore they that were scattered abroad went everywhere preaching the word. Then Philip went down to the city of Samaria, and preached Christ unto them; And the people with one accord gave heed unto those things which Philip spake, hearing and seeing the miracles which he did. And there was great Joy in that city: But when they believed Philip preaching the things concerning the kingdom of God and the name of Jesus Christ, they were baptised, both men and women. Then Simon himself believed also; and when he was baptised, he continued with Philip, and wondered beholding the miracles and signs which were done. And they, when they had testified and preached the word of God, returned to Jerusalem, and preached the gospel in many villages of Samaritans. (Acts 8:4–6, 8, 12–13, 25)

Friends, we can deduce from this that God uses evangelism to baptize and disciple people into his kingdom. The apostle Paul left an indelible mark on the heavenly discipleship program of God. What was the secret behind the colossal success of Paul's apostolic ministry?

Simple! He zealously employed the divine art of evangelism to record an enviable level of breakthroughs in his day. Paul was so completely sold on the Lord's discipleship program that he said a curse was upon him if he preached not the gospel. He turned every house and available forum into a platform to preach and save souls for the kingdom. Read Paul's confirmation of this.

> For necessity is laid upon me, yea woe is unto me, if I preach not the gospel: for if I do this willingly, I have a reward: but if against my will, a dispensation of the gospel is committed unto me. and unto the Jews I became a Jew, that I might gain the Jews: to them that are under the law, that I might gain them that are under the law: To them that are without the law, as without law, (being not without law to God, but under the law to Christ) that I might gain them that are without law. To the weak became I as weak, that I might gain the weak: I am made all things to all men, that I might by all means save some. (1 Corinthians 9:16, 17, 20–22)

> Now while Paul waited for them at Athens, his Spirit was stirred in him, when he saw the city wholly given to idolatry. Therefore disputed he in the synagogue with the Jews, and with the devout persons, and in the market daily with them that met him. Howbeit certain men clave unto him, and believed: among the which was Dionysius, the areopagite, and a woman named Damaris, and others with them. (Acts 17:16, 17, 34)

> And he departed thence, and entered into a certain man's house, named Justus, one that worshiped God, whose house joined hard to the synagogue: And Crispus, the chief ruler of the synagogue, believed on the Lord with all his house; and many of the Corinthians hearing believed and were baptised. (Acts 18:7–8)

It is gratifying to note that the Lord complements our committed discipleship efforts with his divine assurance and support. He provides all the necessary divine and physical resources to facilitate the work. When God leads and directs, he adequately provides.

> Then spake the Lord to Paul in the night by a vision, be not afraid, but speak, and hold not thy peace: for I am with thee, for I have much people in this city: and he continued there a year and six months, teaching the word of God among them. (Acts 18:9–11)

By the ministry of the Word and soul-winning, the apostle Peter preached the Word to Cornelius, his household, and his neighbors. God glorified his holy name in the lives of these and saved and discipled them into his heavenly kingdom. Their conversion and subsequent salvation was effected by the Holy Spirit through Peter. Friends, God is waiting earnestly to use you to save and disciple souls. He knows where lost souls are. Make yourselves available, and He will definitely use you to discover and disciple these lost souls into his glorious kingdom.

> There was a certain man in Caesarea called Cornelius, a centurion of the band called the Italian band; a

devout man, and one that feared God with all his house, which gave much alms to the people, and prayed to God always: and the morrow after they entered into Caesarea. And Cornelius waited for them, and had together his kinsmen and near friends. And as he talked with him, and found many that where come together: immediately therefore I sent to thee; and thou hast well done that thou art come. Now therefore are we all here present before God to hear all things that are commanded thee of God; then Peter opened his mouth; and said of a truth I perceive that God is no respecter of persons; but in every nation he that feareth Him, and worketh righteousness, is accepted with Him. The word of God which GOD sent unto the children of Israel, preaching peace by Jesus Christ; (He is the Lord of all). That word, I say, ye know, which was published throughout all Judaea, and began from Galilee, after the baptism which John preached; and he commanded us to preach unto the people, and to testify that it is he which was ordained of God to be judge of quick and dead: while Peter yet spake these words, the Holy Ghost fell upon them which heard the word. And he commanded them to be baptised in the name of the Lord. Then prayed they him to tarry certain days. (Acts 10:1–2, 33–37, 42, 44, 48)

Acts is replete with undeniable works of discipleship by the apostles and disciples of old through the art of evangelism. It is of paramount importance that discernible and provable methods were masterfully employed by the disciples; some of these methods, however, are similar to the present-day concepts of soul-winning. We are fortunate to be living in a prophetic age in which the Lord has made available to us more-refined strategies that will enable us to record astonishing breakthroughs in ministry. This will no doubt polish as well as add beauty to the discipleship work we offer the Lord. Brethren, we must realize that God expects a higher standard of consecration, commitment, faithfulness, and success in our discipleship. Common sense teaches us that any idea or system matures as it ages; God expects nothing less than this.

> But the path of the just is as the shining light, that shineth more and more unto the perfect day. (Proverbs 4:18)

Methods for Evangelism or Soul-Winning

In the days of the disciples of the old apostolic order, souls were won and discipled into God's kingdom through evangelistic crusades in cities, regions, and countries.

> And when they had preached the gospel to that city, and had taught many, they returned again to Lystra, and to Iconium, and Antioch, confirming the souls of the disciples, and exhorting them to continue in the faith, and that we must through much tribulation, enter into the kingdom of God: and when they had ordained them elders in every church, and had prayed with fasting, they commended them to the Lord, on whom they believed. (Acts 14:21–23)

In 1994, the Lord used evangelist Billy Graham as a human vessel to set Japan aflame with the fire of evangelism through countrywide evangelistic crusades, and as a result, many people were saved and brought into God's kingdom. In 1904, Wales experienced a great spiritual revival; the Spirit of the Lord swiftly moved across the nation like a tornado. God used Evan Roberts mightily to bring about tremendous revivals that awakened dead and cold churches. He was the messenger God used to perfect this discipleship work that spread to Scotland, other parts of Great Britain, Europe, and beyond. This great revival saw many people saved and converted to the wonderful kingdom of God.

These evangelistic efforts required few or no church formalities or other wasted activities that pervade our churches today. God saved and restored sinners, and souls in the thousands willingly joined these revived churches that had been dead to the Holy Spirit. This shows the paramount importance and power of preaching the Word of God with the aid of the Holy Spirit.

Dr. Oswald J. Smith, in his book *The Revival we need*, shed more light on this when he wrote,

> In the year 1835, Titus Coan landed on the shore belt of Hawaii. On his[4] first tour multitudes flocked to hear him; they thronged him so that he had scarcely time to eat. Once he preached three times before he had a chance to take breakfast. He felt that God

---

[4] Oswald J. Smith, The Revival we need, New York, The Christian Alliance Publishing Company, 1925, Chapter 4, page 1.

was strangely at work. In 1837 the slumbering fires broke out. Nearly the whole population became an audience.

He was ministering to 15,000 people. Unable to reach them they came to him, and settled down to a two years' camp meeting. There was not an hour, day or night when an audience from 2,000 to 6,000 would not rally to the signal of the bell. There was trembling, weeping, sobbing and loud crying for mercy, sometimes too loud for the preacher to be heard and in hundreds of cases his hearers fell in a swoon. Some would cry out, 'the two-edged sword is cutting me to pieces."

The wicked scoffer who came to make sport dropped like a dog and cried, "God has struck me." Once while preaching in the open field to 2000 people, a man cried out, "What must I do to be saved?" and prayed the publican's prayer, and the entire congregation took up the cry for mercy. For half an hour Mr Coan could get no chance to speak, but had to stand still and see God work. Quarrels were made up, drunkards reclaimed, adulterers converted, and murderers revealed and pardoned. Thieves returned stolen property. And sins of a life time were renounced. In one year 5,244 joined the church. There were 1, 705 baptised on one Sunday. And 2,400 sat down at the Lord's Table, once sinners of the blackest type, and now saints of God. And when

Mr Coan left he had himself received and baptised 11,960 persons. [5]

Brethren, God is expecting us to finish and perfect this discipleship work that will surpass the work performed by these human instruments. This is very much achievable if we effectively use modern strategies available to us. Through television and radio crusades, improved open-field crusades, readable handbills and posters, books, gifts, tracts, films, and other methods, we could add a gleaming photo finish to our discipleship work we offer to the Lord for committed soul-winning.

It is of paramount importance to stress here that though the methods may change, the message of the gospel is unchanged. Jesus—the crucified, the hope of glory and absolute restoration—must continue to be the objective of our discipleship work. Read the apostle Paul on this point.

> What is my reward then? Verily, that when I preach the gospel, I may make the gospel of Christ without charge, that I abuse not my power in the gospel. For through I be free from all men, yet have I made myself servant unto all, that I might gain the more. (Acts 9:18–19)

Paul was giving the same message but employing different methods acceptable to the Lord.

---

[5]   Oswald J. Smith, The Revival we need, New York, The Christian Alliance Publishing Company, 1925, Chapter 4, page 1.

> Now I beseech you, brethren by the name of our
> Lord Jesus Christ, that ye all speak the same thing and
> that there be no divisions among you: but that ye be
> perfectly joined together in the same mind and in the
> same judgement. (1 Corinthians 1:10)

Brethren, we must not in the name of soul-winning gather vagabonds
and criminals who are unwilling to be changed by the Holy Spirit,
unsanctified and uncircumcised in the spirit and flesh for the heavenly
kingdom. Not all who shout "Lord, Lord" shall enter the kingdom.
Nothing that defiles will gain entrance into our Father's heaven.

> Not everyone that saith unto me, Lord, Lord, shall
> enter into the kingdom of heaven; but he that doeth the
> will of my Father which is in heaven. (Matthew 7:21)

> And there shall in no wise enter into it anything that
> defilleth, neither whatsoever worketh abomination,
> or maketh a lie: but they which are written in the
> Lamb's book of life. (Revelation 21:27)

We must lay a solid apostolic foundation for our converts God had
helped us win to sustain their hard-earned salvation. This in turn
will put a divine seal of approval on our discipleship efforts.

Church Planting and Networking

> I have planted, Apollo's watered; but God gave the
> increase. (1 Corinthians 3:6)

Church planting is the main divine method God has devised to perfect his discipleship program. It is the foundation on which other methods of discipleship are anchored. The word *church* has its origin in the Greek word *ecclessia*, which means the called out or the chosen ones. The church represents the gathering of the redeemed children of God through the splendid finished work, Jesus, perfected on the cross of Calvary. Jesus became the head and originator of the church of God on earth.

> And I say also unto thee, that thou art Peter, and upon this rock I will build my church; and the gates of hell shall not prevail against it. And I will give unto thee the keys of the kingdom of heaven: and whatsoever thou shalt bind on earth shall be bound in heaven: and whatsoever thou shalt loose on earth shall be loosed in heaven. (Matthew 16:18–19)

The apostle Paul presented this revelation this way.

> According as he hath chosen us in him before the foundation of the world, that we should be holy and without blame before him in love. Having predestinated us unto the adoption of children by Jesus Christ to himself, according to the good pleasure of his will. That in the dispensation of the fullness of times he might gather together in one all things in Christ, both which are in heaven, and which are on earth; even in him: And hath put all things under his feet, and gave him to be the head over all things to the church. (Ephesians 1:4, 5, 10, 22)

Brethren, God has a very good reason for establishing his church. He cannot relate with man physically on earth for the simple reason that his glory and holiness are so awesome and dazzling that no one could ever approach him.

> Who only hath immortality, dwelling in the light which no man can approach unto; whom no man hath seen, nor can see: to whom be honour and power everlasting. Amen. (1 Timothy 6:16)

> Touching the Almighty, we cannot find him out: he is excellent in power, and in judgment, and in plenty of justice: he will not afflict. Men do therefore fear him: he respecteth not any that are wise of heart. (Job 37:23–24)

The children of Israel could not withstand the awesome glory of God when he came down to Mount Sinai from his holy throne to communicate with them. They rather fearfully beckoned Moses to act as their go-between.

> And the Lord said unto Moses, Lo, I come unto thee in a thick cloud, that the people may hear when I speak with thee, and believe thee for ever. And Moses told the words of the people unto the Lord. And it came to pass on the third day in the morning, that there were thunders and lightings, and a thick cloud upon the mount, and the voice of the trumpet exceeding loud; so that all the people that was in the camp trembled. And the Lord said unto Moses, Go

down, charge the people, lest they break through unto the Lord to gaze, and many of them perish. (Exodus 19:9, 19, 21)

The church remains the best forum for God to communicate to individuals to save and adopt them into his heavenly family. The church is the voice of God on earth and brings out the purpose of God for his people, which is discipleship and the perfection of the body of Christ, the disciples of Christ.

Moreover whom he did predestinate, them he also called: and whom he called, them he also justified: and whom he justified, them he also glorified. (Romans 8:30)

God is in the business of church planting to reach the unreached for the salvation of their souls from bondage to the Devil. It is in his end-time prophetic agenda to expand his kingdom by planting more churches: He accomplished this objective in the old apostolic church era by using the apostles and church workers.

Thus saith the Lord of hosts; Again in this place, which is desolate without man and without beast, and in all the cities thereof, shall be an habitation of shepherds causing their flocks to lie down. In the cities of the mountains, in the cities of the vale, and in the cities of the south, and in the land of Benjamin, and in the places about Jerusalem, and in the cities of Judah, shall the flocks pass again under the hands of him that telleth them, saith the Lord. In those days shall Judah be saved, and Jerusalem shall dwell safely: and this is the name wherewith she shall be called, The Lord our righteousness. For thus saith the Lord; David shall never want a man to sit upon the throne of the house of Israel; Neither shall the priests the Levites want a man before me to offer burnt offerings, and to kindle meat offerings, and to do sacrifice continually. Thus saith the Lord; If ye can break my covenant of the day, and my covenant of the night, and that there should not be day and night in their season; Then may also my covenant be broken with David my servant, that he should not have a son to reign upon his throne; and with the Levites the priests, my ministers. As the host of heaven cannot be numbered, neither the sand of the sea measured: so will I multiply the seed of David my servant, and the Levites that minister unto me. (Jeremiah 33:12, 13, 16–18, 20–22)

Prophetically, the revelation God gave to Jeremiah was that he would raise shepherds, pastors, to plant the branches of his church with particular visions and missions to save and disciple lost souls and expand his divine kingdom. The word *shepherd* in the above passage implies the Levites, pastors with apostolic anointing God commissioned to plant branches of his church on earth to prepare his saints for rapture into the heavenly kingdom.

And I will give you pastors according to mine heart, which shall feed you with knowledge and understanding. And it shall come to pass, when ye be multiplied and increased in the land, in those days, saith the Lord, they shall say no more, The ark of the covenant of the Lord: neither shall it come to mind: neither shall they remember it; neither shall they visit it; neither shall that be done any more. (Jeremiah 3:15–16)

The prophet Ezekiel put this revelation thus.

As the holy flock, as the flock of Jerusalem in her solemn feasts; so shall the waste cities be filled with flocks of men: and they shall know that I am the Lord. (Ezekiel 36:38)

One may be tempted to ask why new churches should be opened when there are existing churches. Brethren, the simple answer is that those saved, called, ordained, and commissioned for the ministry work have disappointed God in great numbers. They have used mundane doctrines and philosophies to pollute the church of God, thus tarnishing God's noble objective of saving and discipling men and women into His heavenly kingdom. He is looking for faithful, obedient, holy, and yielding people to ordain and commission into church planting programs to achieve his divine aim.

Many pastors have destroyed the vineyard, they have trodden my portion under foot, they have made my pleasant portion a desolate wilderness; they have made it desolate, and being desolate it mourneth unto me: the whole land is made desolate because no man layeth it to heart. (Ezekiel 12:10–11)

And the word of the Lord came unto me, saying; son of man, prophesy against the shepherds of Israel, prophesy, and say unto them; thus saith the Lord God unto the shepherds of Israel that do feed themselves! Should not the shepherds feed the flocks? Ye eat the fat, and ye cloth you with the wool, ye kill them that are fed: but ye feed not the flocks. And they were scattered because there is no shepherd; and they became meat to all the beasts of the field; when they were scattered: my sheep wondered through all the mountains, and upon all the face of the earth, and none did search or seek after them: therefore, o ye shepherds, hear the word of the Lord: thus saith the Lord, God: Behold I am against the shepherds: and I will require my flock at their hand, and cause them to cease from feeding the flock; neither shall the shepherds feed themselves anymore: for I will deliver my flock from their mouth, that they may not be meat for them; and I will set up one shepherd over them, and he shall feed, even my servant David, he shall feed them, and he shall be their shepherd. (Ezekiel 34:1–3, 5, 6, 9, 10, 23)

Many pastors have polluted the sanctuary of God; this has made the majority of the children of God wander hills and mountains (i.e., all church gatherings that lack the presence of God). Brethren, it is from the confusion on these polluted mountains and hills, that is, churches and ministries, that God will bring to his scattered people true pastors, saviors, and messengers to lead his children with the aid of different ministries into the body of Christ.

And saviours shall come up on mount Zion to judge the mount of Esau; and the kingdom shall be the Lord's. (Obadiah 1:21)

And I will turn your feasts into mourning, and all your songs into lamentation; and I will bring up sackcloth upon all loins, and baldness upon every head; and I will make it as the mourning of an only son, and the end thereof as a bitter day. Behold, the days come, saith the Lord God, that I will send a famine in the land, not a famine of bread, nor a thirst for water, but of hearing the words of the Lord: And they shall wander from sea to sea, and from the north even to the east, they shall run to and fro to seek the word of the Lord, and shall not find it. (Amos 8:10–12)

Behold, the eyes of the Lord God are upon the sinful kingdom, and I will destroy it from off the face of the earth; saving that I will not utterly destroy the house of Jacob, saith the Lord. For, lo, I will command, and I will sift the house of Israel among all nations, like as corn is sifted in a sieve, yet shall not the least grain fall upon the earth. All the sinners of my people shall die by the sword, which say, The evil shall not overtake nor prevent us. In that day will I raise up the tabernacle of David that is fallen, and close up the breaches thereof; and I will raise up his ruins, and I will build it as in the days of old: And I will bring again the captivity of my people of Israel, and they shall build the waste cities, and inhabit them; and they shall plant vineyards, and drink the wine thereof; they shall also make gardens, and eat the fruit of them. (Amos 9:8–11, 14)

Church Networking

The unity of the body of Christ is very important to God, the owner and planter of the church. He loves his church and consequently derives pleasure in the oneness of the body of Christ.

> Neither pray I for these alone, but for them also which shall believe on me through their word; That they all may be one; as thou, Father, art in me, and I in thee, that they also may be one in us: that the world may believe that thou hast sent me. And the glory which thou gavest me I have given them; that they may be one, even as we are one. (John 17:20–22)

Church networking among believing disciples makes this unity possible and available. Unity increases the strength of the disciples of Christ and improves the quality of discipleship.

> Behold, how good and how pleasant it is for brethren to dwell together in unity! It is like the precious ointment upon the head that ran down upon the beard even Aaron's beard: that went down to the skirts of his garments; as the dew of Hermon, and as the dew that descended upon the mountains of Zion:

for there the Lord commanded the blessing, even life
for evermore. (Psalm 133:1–3)

The apostle Paul caught this revelation.

> That there should be no schism in the body; but
> that the members should have the same care one for
> another. And whether one member suffers, all the
> members suffer with it; or one member be honored,
> all the members rejoice with it. Now ye are the body
> of Christ, and members in particular. (1 Corinthians
> 12:25–27)

Simply defined, church networking is the divine art of allowing
the churches of God with a common vision, mission, purpose, and
doctrines to work in harmony with each other. This will in turn
make way for the emergence of God-centered discipleship. Church
networking encourages joint fellowship and true worship of God
among believers. It gives birth to a lively, acceptable liturgy. The
church is God's redemptive agent for reconciling the world to himself.

> Till we all come in the unity of the faith, and of the
> knowledge of the Son of God, unto a perfect man,
> unto the measure of the stature of the fullness of
> Christ. (Ephesians 4:13)

The churches need each other if they honestly wish to allow God to
use them to accomplish his divine purpose of building the church
on earth. God had made them mutually dependent on one another;
what one lacks, the other can willingly and humbly supply.

The churches of the New Testament period worked with each other happily. Though they retained their individual missions and visions, revelations from the Lord, they needed one another and very much related to each other in the work of the kingdom. This unquestionably made them encourage and help each other increase and improve discipleship. This networking also enabled them to sustain their fellowship with God and perfect their discipleship work they offered to the Lord, and subsequently, they had a better experience of God.

Brethren, divine fellowship among the Christian disciples makes for better experiences, and it shapes and creates opportunities for new beginnings. This in turn makes room for better divine blessings as a greater number of churches network together in the kingdom of God.

Church planting makes room for Godly sharing and oneness and gives birth to a greater form of Christian discipleship and mutual encouragement in these churches: This undoubtedly will attract and draw a watching but directionless world to Christ and his church.

> And they continued steadfastly in the apostles' doctrine and fellowship, and in breaking of bread, and in prayers. And fear came upon every soul: and many wonders and signs were done by the apostles. And all that believed were together, and had all things common; And they, continuing daily with one accord in the temple, and breaking bread from house to house, did eat their meat with gladness and singleness of heart, praising God, and having favour with all the people. And the Lord added to the church daily such as should be saved. (Acts 2:42–47)

The New Testament churches established and sustained cooperative and working relationships with each other to provide for each other's lack, and they taught the doctrines of Christ and sustained kingdom works. The Scriptures told us how the churches in Achaia and Macedonia sent provisions to the poor Christian believers in Jerusalem.

> When so ever I take my journey in Spain, I will come to you; for I trust to see you in my journey, and to be brought on my way thither-ward by you, if first I be somewhat filled with your company; But now I go unto Jerusalem to minister unto the saints; for it hath pleased them of Macedonia and Achaia to make a certain contribution for it hath pleased them verily; and their debtors they are. For if the Gentiles have been made partakers of their spiritual things, their duty is also to minister unto them in carnal things. (Acts 15:24–27)

t is imperative to note that the church at Antioch was mission-minded. Its members decided to play active role in the Great Commission of winning a lost, sinful world to God. They helped each other and exchanged ideas and ministers.

As they ministered to the Lord, and fasted, the Holy Ghost said, Separate me Barnabas and Saul for the work whereunto I have called them. And when they had fasted and prayed, and laid their hands on them, they sent them away. (Acts 13:2–3)

Brethren, we need to be very careful and watchful when networking with other churches. Though so many benefits abound in cooperating with each other, it is advisable not to network with churches that do not follow the undiluted doctrines of Christ, upon which his church was built and revolves. Quality networking results in quality discipleship and fellowship.

> Look to yourselves, that we lose not those things which we have wrought, but that we receive a full reward. Whosoever transgresseth, and abideth not in the doctrine of Christ, hath not God. He that abideth in the doctrine of Christ, he hath both the Father and the Son. If there come any unto you, and bring not this doctrine, receive him not into your house, neither bid him God speed: For he that biddeth him God speed is partaker of his evil deeds. (2 John 8–11)

The apostle John confirmed this.

> And I heard another voice from heaven, saying, Come out of her, my people, that ye be not partakers of her sins, and that ye receive not of her plagues. For her sins have reached unto heaven, and God hath remembered her iniquities. (Revelation 18:4–5)

> Go ye therefore, and teach all nations, baptizing them in the name of the Father, and of the Son, and of the Holy Ghost: Teaching them to observe all things whatsoever I have commanded you: and, lo, I am with you always, even unto the end of the world. Amen. (Matthew 28:19–20)

The Costs of Discipleship

The costs of discipleship are the sacrifices disciples have to make to do the work of discipleship that has been committed into the hands of the church. God demands total and undivided attention when he calls us into his discipleship work. Paul, Peter, and other disciples of Christ made costly sacrifices to complete their kingdom works. David the psalmist, writing under the power of the Holy Spirit, reinforced this revealed truth.

> Gather my saints together unto me; those that have made a covenant with me by sacrifice. (Psalms 50:5)

Jesus emphatically told his disciples in Luke that a true disciple was one who was wise enough to count the cost of discipleship, following Christ, before embarking on it. Discipleship is a lifelong experience that demands patience, skill, faithfulness, and submission to the Lord.

> And they all with one consent began to make excuse. The first said unto him, I have bought a piece of ground, and I must needs go and see it: I pray thee have me excused. And another said, I have bought five yoke of oxen, and I go to prove them: I pray thee have me excused. And another said, I have married a wife, and therefore I cannot come. So that servant came, and shewed his lord these things. Then the master of the house being angry said to his servant, Go out quickly into the streets and lanes of the city, and bring in hither the poor, and the maimed, and the halt, and the blind. And the servant said, Lord,

it is done as thou hast commanded, and yet there is room. And the lord said unto the servant, Go out into the highways and hedges, and compel them to come in, that my house may be filled. For I say unto you, That none of those men which were bidden shall taste of my supper. And there went great multitudes with him: and he turned, and said unto them. If any man come to me, and hate not his father, and mother, and wife, and children, and brethren, and sisters, yea, and his own life also, he cannot be my disciple. And whosoever doth not bear his cross, and come after me, cannot be my disciple. For which of you, intending to build a tower, sitteth not down first, and counteth the cost, whether he have sufficient to finish it? Lest haply, after he hath laid the foundation, and is not able to finish it, all that behold it begin to mock him, Saying, This man began to build, and was not able to finish. (Luke 14:18–30)

The cost of discipleship can briefly be summarized under three headings.

1. Total Surrender and Consecration

God expects absolute submission and faithfulness of his disciples. He wants us to consider our trust in him over any other consideration. Consecration is a true mark of discipleship.

No man can serve two masters: for either he will hate the one, and love the other; or else he will hold to the one, and despise the other. Ye cannot serve God and mammon. But seek ye first the kingdom of God, and his righteousness; and all these things shall be added unto you. (Matthew 6:24, 33)

Submit yourselves therefore to God. Resist the devil, and he will flee from you. Draw nigh to God, and he will draw nigh to you. Cleanse your hands, ye sinners; and purify your hearts, ye double minded. Humble yourselves in the sight of the Lord, and he shall lift you up. (James 4:7, 8, 10)

2. Willingness and Resolve to Bear a Cross

The willingness and strong resolve to carry a cross and follow God is another defined hallmark of true discipleship. The cross involves the compulsory Christian sufferings, persecutions, temptations, and trials a Christian believer must have to undergo as the costly price of following Christ.

When thou passest through the waters, I will be with thee; and through the rivers, they shall not overflow thee: when thou walkest through the fire, thou shalt not be burned; neither shall the flame kindle upon thee. For I am the Lord thy God, the Holy One of Israel, thy Saviour: I gave Egypt for thy ransom, Ethiopia and Seba for thee. (Isaiah 43:2–3)

Forasmuch then as Christ hath suffered for us in the flesh, arm yourselves likewise with the same mind:

for he that hath suffered in the flesh hath ceased from sin; That he no longer should live the rest of his time in the flesh to the lusts of men, but to the will of God. Beloved, think it not strange concerning the fiery trial which is to try you, as though some strange thing happened unto you: But rejoice, inasmuch as ye are partakers of Christ's sufferings; that, when his glory shall be revealed, ye may be glad also with exceeding joy. If ye be reproached for the name of Christ, happy are ye; for the spirit of glory and of God resteth upon you: on their part he is evil spoken of, but on your part he is glorified. But let none of you suffer as a murderer, or as a thief, or as an evildoer, or as a busybody in other men's matters. Yet if any man suffer as a Christian, let him not be ashamed; but let him glorify God on this behalf. For the time is come that judgment must begin at the house of God: and if it first begin at us, what shall the end be of them that obey not the gospel of God? And if the righteous scarcely be saved, where shall the ungodly and the sinner appear? Wherefore let them that suffer according to the will of God commit the keeping of their souls to him in well doing, as unto a faithful Creator. (1 Peter 4:1–2, 12–19)

And whosoever doth not bear his cross, and come after me, cannot be my disciple. (Luke 14:27)

For the which cause I also suffer these things: nevertheless I am not ashamed: for I know whom

I have believed, and am persuaded that he is able to keep that which I have committed unto him against that day. (2 Timothy 1:12)

My brethren, count it all joy when ye fall into divers temptations; Knowing this, that the trying of your faith worketh patience. (James 1:2–3)

Blessed are ye, when men shall revile you, and persecute you, and shall say all manner of evil against you falsely, for my sake. (Matthew 5:11)

But watch thou in all things, endure afflictions, do the work of an evangelist, make full proof of thy ministry. (2 Timothy 4:5)

3. Total Forsaking of Old Ways

So likewise, whosoever he be of you that forsaketh not all that he hath, he cannot be my disciple. (Luke 14:33)

Friends, following Jesus Christ, which true discipleship entails, demands total abandonment of old, sinful ways, thoughts, and actions. God expects from true disciples a complete rejection of every form of sin and worldly desire.

Love not the world, neither the things that are in the world. If any man love the world, the love of the Father is not in him. For all that is in the world, the lust of the flesh, and the lust of the eyes, and the pride of life, is not of the Father, but is of the world. And the world passeth away, and the lust thereof: but he that doeth the will of God abideth for ever. (1 John 2:15–17)

Peter, John, and the disciples left all to follow Jesus, and this earned them divine approval for their discipleship work.

Then Peter began to say unto him, Lo, we have left all, and have followed thee. And Jesus answered and said, Verily I say unto you, There is no man that hath left house, or brethren, or sisters, or father, or mother, or wife, or children, or lands, for my sake, and the gospel's, but he shall receive an hundredfold now in this time, houses, and brethren, and sisters, and mothers, and children, and lands, with persecutions; and in the world to come eternal life. But many that are first shall be last; and the last first. (Mark 10:28–31)

Forsaking all for true discipleship involves painful sacrifices. These sacrifices, however, open hidden doors of opportunities for divine ministry and put a divine seal on true discipleship. When Noah offered acceptable sacrifices, God opened up a door of opportunity for him to get out of the ark of salvation and launch into another beginning or discipleship walk with God.

And Noah builded an altar unto the LORD; and took of every clean beast, and of every clean fowl, and offered burnt offerings on the altar. While the earth remaineth, seedtime and harvest, and cold and heat, and summer and winter, and day and night shall not cease. (Genesis 8:20, 22)

And God blessed Noah and his sons, and said unto them, Be fruitful, and multiply, and replenish the earth. And you, be ye fruitful, and multiply; bring forth abundantly in the earth, and multiply therein. (Genesis 9:1, 7)

CHAPTER 7

The Role of Prophecy and Revelation in Discipleship

Where there is no vision, the people perish.

—Proverbs 29:18

The strategic role of prophecy in discipleship can never be wished away; prophecy plays a pivotal role in the end-time discipleship program of the kingdom of God. It gives divine direction and insights desperately required to successfully initiate, complete, and perfect the discipleship work God has committed into our hands.

Paul and Barnabas were accomplishing the work of the Great Commission with the church in Antioch when, in a prayer and fasting session, the instrument of prophecy came into play, separating Paul and Barnabas into different mission fields. This action enabled the church to reach other lands and peoples for the kingdom of God.

> Now there were in the church that was at Antioch certain prophets and teachers; as Barnabas, and Simeon that was called Niger, and Lucius of Cyrene, and Manaen, which had been brought up with Herod

the tetrarch, and Saul. As they ministered to the Lord, and fasted, the Holy Ghost said, Separate me Barnabas and Saul for the work whereunto I have called them. And when they had fasted and prayed, and laid their hands on them, they sent them away. So they, being sent forth by the Holy Ghost, departed unto Seleucia; and from thence they sailed to Cyprus. And when they were at Salamis, they preached the word of God in the synagogues of the Jews: and they had also John to their minister. (Acts 13:1–5)

The spirit of prophecy brings illumination and clarity for effective and God-led discipleship work in the church. It gives clear-cut revelational knowledge of God's purpose and direction that propels the wheels of discipleship programs. In Acts 8, Philip was effectively conducting an evangelistic outreach when the spirit of prophecy came upon him and changed the course of his evangelistic ministry. He was led to Gaza to open the door of salvation to Africa by the conversion of the Ethiopian eunuch. This Ethiopian carried this kingdom fire into Ethiopia and by extension the African continent.

Therefore they that were scattered abroad went every where preaching the word. Then Philip went down to the city of Samaria, and preached Christ unto them. And the people with one accord gave heed unto those things which Philip spake, hearing and seeing the miracles which he did. And the angel of the Lord spake unto Philip, saying, Arise, and go toward the south unto the way that goeth down from Jerusalem unto Gaza, which is desert. And he arose and went:

and, behold, a man of Ethiopia, an eunuch of great authority under Candace queen of the Ethiopians, who had the charge of all her treasure, and had come to Jerusalem for to worship, Was returning, and sitting in his chariot read Esaias the prophet. Then the Spirit said unto Philip, Go near, and join thyself to this chariot. And Philip ran thither to him, and heard him read the prophet Esaias, and said, Understandest thou what thou readest? And he said, How can I, except some man should guide me? And he desired Philip that he would come up and sit with him. Then Philip opened his mouth, and began at the same scripture, and preached unto him Jesus. And Philip said, If thou believest with all thine heart, thou mayest. And he answered and said, I believe that Jesus Christ is the Son of God. And he commanded the chariot to stand still: and they went down both into the water, both Philip and the eunuch; and he baptized him. And when they were come up out of the water, the Spirit of the Lord caught away Philip, that the eunuch saw him no more: and he went on his way rejoicing. But Philip was found at Azotus: and passing through he preached in all the cities, till he came to Caesarea. (Acts 8:4–6, 26–31, 35, 37–40)

When we allow the spirit of prophecy to initiate, order, shape, and complete the discipleship work of God's kingdom, the apparent result is a well-defined, directed, purpose-driven, and divinely approved discipleship. The apostle Paul was somehow undecided and needed divine direction as to where to continue his ministry when the spirit of prophecy directed him to Macedonia. As he obeyed, he accomplished great and astonishing breakthroughs. The Spirit of the Lord knows where and how we need to conduct our discipleship works and thus will enable and direct us according to the divine will of God. God wants us to respond to the promptings of the Spirit and to submit completely.

> Now when they had gone throughout Phrygia and the region of Galatia, and were forbidden of the Holy Ghost to preach the word in Asia, After they were come to Mysia, they assayed to go into Bithynia: but the Spirit suffered them not. And they passing by Mysia came down to Troas. And a vision appeared to Paul in the night; There stood a man of Macedonia, and prayed him, saying, Come over into Macedonia, and help us. And after he had seen the vision, immediately we endeavoured to go into Macedonia, assuredly gathering that the Lord had called us for to preach the gospel unto them. Therefore loosing from Troas, we came with a straight course to Samothracia, and the next day to Neapolis; And from thence to Philippi, which is the chief city of that part of Macedonia, and a colony: and we were in that city abiding certain days. (Acts 16:6–12)

The apostle Paul recognized and treasured the spirit of the prophecy so much that he urged the Christian brethren at Ephesus to pray God to grant him the Spirit of prophecy. This help shaped and flavored the apostolic and discipleship work he carried out for the Lord.

> And for me, that utterance [prophetic direction] may
> be given unto me, that I may open my mouth boldly,
> to make known the mystery of the gospel, for which
> I am an ambassador in bonds: that therein I may speak
> boldly, as I ought to speak. (Ephesians 6:19–20)

Moses received a distinct prophetic blueprint from the Lord before creating his discipleship program for the Lord. He obtained and walked in the Spirit of prophecy and thus recorded astonishing breakthroughs in the prophetic ministry God committed into his hands. On Mount Sinai, God gave Moses a prophetic blueprint for the construction of a sanctuary on which to disciple the nation of Israel properly into his kingdom. He warned him to strictly stick to this heavenly standard just as he was instructing his servants in this present apostolic dispensation.

> And the LORD came down upon mount Sinai, on the
> top of the mount: and the LORD called Moses up to the
> top of the mount; and Moses went up. (Exodus 19:20)

> And let them make me a sanctuary; that I may dwell
> among them. According to all that I shew thee, after
> the pattern of the tabernacle, and the pattern of all
> the instruments thereof, even so shall ye make it. And
> look that thou make them after their pattern, which
> was shewed thee in the mount. (Exodus 25: 8–9, 40)

Moses obeyed and stuck to this divine pattern and obtained great success in ministry. He refused to be distracted or allow his environment to influence or shape his discipleship work.

Thus did Moses according to all that the Lord commanded him, so did he. And it came to pass in the first month in the second year, on the first day of the month, that the tabernacle was reared up. And he reared up the court round about the tabernacle and the altar, and set up the hanging of the court gate. So Moses finished the work. Then a cloud covered the tent of the congregation, and the glory of the Lord filled the tabernacle. (Exodus 40:16–17, 33–34)

God is still instructing the church to stick to the New Testament prophetic pattern in building the discipleship work of the Great Commission. God's pattern in this New Testament era is the cross of Calvary. That is the true, divinely approved pattern each discipleship work should be built on in the church. It is Christ's finished and perfected work of grace on the cross. Jesus realized this prophetic blueprint when he said,

And as Moses lifted up the serpent in the wilderness, even so must the Son of man be lifted up: That whosoever believeth in him should not perish, but have eternal life. (John 3:14–15)

And I, if I be lifted up from the earth, will draw all men unto me. (John 12:32)

God expects us to build and pattern our discipleship on this model or risk building castles in the air. Jesus emphatically warned the church that unless its members took up his cross and followed him, they were not his disciples. Against this backdrop, the church must strive to conform to this discipleship pattern.

> And whosoever doth not bear his cross, and come after me, cannot be my disciple. (Luke 14:27)

The apostle Paul captured this revelation in this light.

> And I, brethren, when I came to you, came not with excellency of speech or of wisdom, declaring unto you the testimony of God. For I determined not to know any thing among you, save Jesus Christ, and him crucified. And I was with you in weakness, and in fear, and in much trembling. And my speech and my preaching was not with enticing words of man's wisdom, but in demonstration of the Spirit and of power: That your faith should not stand in the wisdom of men, but in the power of God. (1 Corinthians 2:1–5)

The spirit of prophecy brings order and stability to the church. It will enable members of the church to test the quality of their discipleship and settle only for that which is good and divinely approved. This will no doubt assist in detecting the work of Satan and his agents who have infiltrated the rank and file of the church. Through discernment, Paul was able to notice the spirit of error, false prophecy, operating in the life of the girl possessed by the evil spirit of divination. He quickly confronted that error, and that won so many converts into the kingdom of God.

And it came to pass, as we went to prayer, a certain damsel possessed with a spirit of divination met us, which brought her masters much gain by soothsaying: The same followed Paul and us, and cried, saying, These men are the servants of the most high God, which shew unto us the way of salvation. And this did she many days. But Paul, being grieved, turned and said to the spirit, I command thee in the name of Jesus Christ to come out of her. And he came out the same hour. And they said, Believe on the Lord Jesus Christ, and thou shalt be saved, and thy house. And they spake unto him the word of the Lord, and to all that were in his house. And he took them the same hour of the night, and washed their stripes; and was baptized, he and all his, straightway. (Acts 16:16–18, 31–33)

The apostle Paul repositioned this divine revealed truth.

Let the prophets speak two or three, and let the other judge. If any thing be revealed to another that sitteth by, let the first hold his peace. For God is not the author of confusion, but of peace, as in all churches of the saints. Let all things be done decently and in order. (1 Corinthians 14:29–30, 33, 40)

Paul also communicated the same revelation to the Christian believers at Thessalonica and enjoined them not to devalue God's spirit of prophecy but to desire it earnestly and allow it space to perfect the work of discipleship of the church.

> Quench not the Spirit [the spirit of prophecy]:
> Despise not prophesyings. Prove all things; hold fast
> that which is good. Abstain from all appearance of
> evil. (1 Thessalonians 5:19–22)

Friends, the spirit of prophecy will help the church detect and remove doctrinal and structural errors in the construction and maintenance of the discipleship work of God's kingdom. This will enable the church to stick, as did Moses and the apostles of the old church order, to the divine pattern and standard God intends. In the discipleship era of the prophet Jeremiah, when Hananiah, the false prophet, tried to pollute the prophetic blueprint God had given Jeremiah to build a heavenly patterned discipleship structure, God quickly helped Jeremiah counter this error. This enabled him to complete the work he had received from the Lord. The present church dispensation must genuinely pray for the true spirit of prophecy to build a qualitative and heaven-approved discipleship.

> And it came to pass the same year, in the beginning
> of the reign of Zedekiah king of Judah, in the fourth
> year, and in the fifth month, that Hananiah the son of
> Azur the prophet, which was of Gibeon, spake unto
> me in the house of the Lord, in the presence of the
> priests and of all the people, saying, thus speaketh the
> Lord of hosts, the God of Israel, saying, I have broken
> the yoke of the king of Babylon. Within two full
> years will I bring again into this place all the vessels
> of the Lord's house, that Nebuchadnezzar king of
> Babylon took away from this place, and carried them
> to Babylon: Then Hananiah the prophet took the

yoke from off the prophet Jeremiah's neck, and brake
it. Then Hananiah the prophet took the yoke from off
the prophet Jeremiah's neck, and brake it. Then the
word of the Lord came unto Jeremiah the prophet,
after that Hananiah the prophet had broken the yoke
from off the neck of the prophet Jeremiah, saying,
go and tell Hananiah, saying, Thus saith the Lord;
Thou hast broken the yokes of wood; but thou shalt
make for them yokes of iron. Then said the prophet
Jeremiah unto Hananiah the prophet, Hear now,
Hananiah; The Lord hath not sent thee; but thou
makest this people to trust in a lie. Therefore thus
saith the Lord; Behold, I will cast thee from off the
face of the earth: this year thou shalt die, because thou
hast taught rebellion against the Lord. So Hananiah
the prophet died the same year in the seventh month.
(Jeremiah 28:1–3, 10, 12–13, 15–17)

The spirit of prophecy comforts and assists the church to learn and
increase progressively in the knowledge and wisdom of God, the
owner and builder of the discipleship work and structures of the
living church. Because God owns this work and intends it to be
carried out, we need to seek and learn his mind and ask for effective
means of accomplishing this glorious work. This is willingly released
through the spirit of prophecy. Jesus told us in John that he had work
given to him by his heavenly Father and that he did nothing of his
own but as the spirit of prophecy led him. He was, as a result, very
successful in the discipleship work he embarked upon. The apostle
Paul captured this revelation thus.

But he that prophesieth speaketh unto men to edification, and exhortation, and comfort. He that speaketh in an unknown tongue edifieth himself; but he that prophesieth edifieth the church. For ye may all prophesy one by one, that all may learn, and all may be comforted. (1 Corinthians 14:3–4, 31)

While Paul was waiting in Athens for Silas and Timothy, he was greatly upset when he noticed how full of idols the city was. So he held discussions in the synagogue with the Jews and with the Gentiles who worshiped God, and also in the public square every day with the people who happened to come by. Certain Epicurean and Stoic teachers also debated with him. Some of them asked, What is this ignorant show-off trying to say?

Others answered, He seems to be talking about foreign gods. They said this because Paul was preaching about Jesus and the resurrection. So they took Paul, brought him before the city council, the Areopagus, and said, We would like to know what this new teaching is that you are talking about. Some of the things we hear you say sound strange to us, and we would like to know what they mean. (For all the citizens of Athens and the foreigners who lived there liked to spend all their time telling and hearing the latest new thing.)

Paul stood up in front of the city council and said, "I see that in every way you Athenians are very religious.

For as I walked through your city and looked at the places where you worship, I found an altar on which is written, 'To an Unknown God.' That which you worship, then, even though you do not know it, is what I now proclaim to you. God, who made the world and everything in it, is Lord of heaven and earth and does not live in temples made by human hands.

Nor does he need anything that we can supply by working for him, since it is he himself who gives life and breath and everything else to everyone. From one human being he created all races of people and made them live throughout the whole earth. He himself fixed beforehand the exact times and the limits of the places where they would live. He did this so that they would look for him, and perhaps find him as they felt around for him. Yet God is actually not far from any one of us; as someone has said, 'In him we live and move and exist.' It is as some of your poets have said, 'We too are his children.'

Since we are God's children, we should not suppose that his nature is anything like an image of gold or silver or stone, shaped by human art and skill. God has overlooked the times when people did not know him, but now he commands all of them everywhere to turn away from their evil ways. For he has fixed a day in which he will judge the whole world with justice by means of a man he has chosen. He has given proof of this to everyone by raising that man from death!

When they heard Paul speak about a raising from death, some of them made fun of him, but others said,We want to hear you speak about this again.And so Paul left the meeting.Some men joined him and believed, among whom was Dionysius, a member of the council; there was also a woman named Damaris, and some other people. (Acts 17:16–34)

Prophecy guarantees God's support and backing that is needed to build heaven-approved discipleship. This divine assurance produces the necessary empowerment and strengthening the church needs for discipleship work. It also puts the divine seal of approval on its work. When God gives disciples assignments, he backs them up with all that is necessary to accomplish the work.

Then spake the Lord to Paul in the night by a vision, Be not afraid, but speak, and hold not thy peace: For I am with thee, and no man shall set on thee to hurt thee: for I have much people in this city. And he continued there a year and six months, teaching the word of God among them. And after he had spent some time there, he departed, and went over all the country of Galatia and Phrygia in order, strengthening all the disciples. (Acts 18:9–11, 23)

Confirming the souls of the disciples, and exhorting them to continue in the faith, and that we must through much tribulation enter into the kingdom of God. (Acts 14:22)

> And Judas and Silas, being prophets also themselves,
> exhorted the brethren with many words, and
> confirmed them. And he went through Syria and
> Cilicia, confirming the churches. (Acts 15:32, 41)

The spirit of prophecy breaks down every satanic gate blocking the hearts and destinies of demon-ravaged and closed lives of all men and women. The Devil, the prince and ruler of this world, has systematically blocked the hearts of people from seeking and living out the will and purpose of God for their lives. He is using all seen and unseen tricks, methods, and distractions to divert people from the gospel of salvation and peace.

> But if our gospel be hid, it is hid to them that are
> lost: In whom the god of this world hath blinded the
> minds of them which believe not, lest the light of the
> glorious gospel of Christ, who is the image of God,
> should shine unto them. For we preach not ourselves,
> but Christ Jesus the Lord; and ourselves your servants
> for Jesus' sake. For God, who commanded the light
> to shine out of darkness, hath shined in our hearts, to
> give the light of the knowledge of the glory of God in
> the face of Jesus Christ. (2 Corinthians 4:3–6)

However, when the spirit of prophecy shows up, every satanic gate of unbelief gives way to the glorious light of the gospel of salvation to shine through the inner recesses of these captives. God, with the instrument of prophecy, enables his messengers to erect and perfect the discipleship works of his kingdom because he sticks to heavenly patterns and standards.

I have also spoken by the prophets [messengers], and
I have multiplied visions, and used similitudes, by the
ministry of the prophets. And by a prophet the Lord
brought Israel out of Egypt, and by a prophet was he
preserved. (Hosea 12:10, 13)

The prophet Amos repositioned this truth in this light.

Surely the Lord God will do nothing, but he revealeth
his secret unto his servants the prophets. (Amos 3:7)

In Ezekiel 37, the Lord took the prophet to the valley of dry bones,
which represented the decayed, unacceptable discipleship structure
of the house of Israel, and commanded him to use the instrument of
prophecy to revive the discipleship work they had earlier offered to
God. Against the backdrop of this prophetic utterance, every grave of
unbelief and sin opened, and a brand-new and approved discipleship
structure emerged.

The hand of the LORD was upon me, and carried
me out in the spirit of the Lord, and set me down in
the midst of the valley which was full of bones, And
caused me to pass by them round about: and, behold,
there were very many in the open valley; and, lo, they
were very dry. And he said unto me, Son of man, can
these bones live? And I answered, O Lord God, thou
knowest. Again he said unto me, Prophesy upon these
bones, and say unto them, O ye dry bones, hear the
word of the Lord. Thus saith the Lord God unto these
bones; Behold, I will cause breath to enter into you,

and ye shall live: So I prophesied as he commanded me, and the breath came into them, and they lived, and stood up upon their feet, an exceeding great army. Then he said unto me, Son of man, these bones are the whole house of Israel: behold, they say, Our bones are dried, and our hope is lost: we are cut off for our parts. Therefore prophesy and say unto them, Thus saith the Lord God; Behold, O my people, I will open your graves, and cause you to come up out of your graves, and bring you into the land of Israel. (Ezekiel 37:1–5, 10–12)

The apostle Paul's prophetic work on the people of Athens converted and changed the discipleship structure of some of the people there. He shifted their focus from their idolatrous worship to following the true God.

While Paul was waiting in Athens for Silas and Timothy, he was greatly upset when he noticed how full of idols the city was. So he held discussions in the synagogue with the Jews and with the Gentiles who worshiped God, and also in the public square every day with the people who happened to come by. Certain Epicurean and Stoic teachers also debated with him. Some of them asked, What is this ignorant show-off trying to say?

Others answered, He seems to be talking about foreign gods. They said this because Paul was preaching about Jesus and the resurrection. So they took Paul, brought him before the city council, the Areopagus, and said, We would like to know what this new teaching is that you are talking about. Some of the things we hear you say sound strange to us, and we would like to know what they mean.(For all the citizens of Athens and the foreigners who lived there liked to spend all their time telling and hearing the latest new thing.)

Paul stood up in front of the city council and said, I see that in every way you Athenians are very religious. And so Paul left the meeting. Some men joined him and believed, among whom was Dionysius, a member of the council; there was also a woman named Damaris, and some other people. (Acts 17:16–22, 33–34)

CHAPTER 8

The Place of Divine Wisdom and Grace in Discipleship

Who is a wise man and endued with knowledge
among you? let him shew out of a good conversation
his works with meekness of wisdom.

—James 3:13

The propagation of the gospel of the kingdom of God is an act of fruitful persuasion that turns sinners away from worldly views and toward heavenly views. It thus requires the divine winning wisdom of God, and that is why Paul always prayed for the spirit of wisdom and grace to be given to him by the Lord.

Friends, the wisdom of God demands us to learn what to do at any time as we build this end-time discipleship program. The church must desire and sustain the enabling grace and wisdom of God to complete the Great Commission. What then is wisdom and grace? According to the *New Oxford Illustrated Dictionary*, wisdom is "being wise; soundness of judgment in matters relating to life and conduct: knowledge, enlightenment, learning." The same dictionary aptly defines *grace* to mean "unmerited favor of God, divine regenerating, inspiring and strengthening influence."

The wisdom of God differs from this definition. The wisdom of God can aptly be defined as the knowledge of God's will and the burning desire to obey and act on it. It demands that we know what to do at any time as we build this end-time discipleship structure.

In Matthew 7, Jesus described a wise man as one who had heard the words of God and made genuine efforts to obey. He encouraged his disciples to continue steadfastly with the word of God ministered to them if they expect God's divine approval.

> Therefore whosoever heareth these sayings of mine, and doeth them, I will liken him unto a wise man, which built his house upon a rock: And the rain descended, and the floods came, and the winds blew, and beat upon that house; and it fell not: for it was founded upon a rock. (Matthew 7:24–25)

> Whosoever cometh to me, and heareth my sayings, and doeth them, I will shew you to whom he is like: He is like a man which built an house, and digged deep, and laid the foundation on a rock: and when the flood arose, the stream beat vehemently upon that house, and could not shake it: for it was founded upon a rock. (Luke 6:47–48)

The carnal wisdom of this wicked life cannot be used in building the discipleship structure because it is full of imperfections and lies.

It is foolishness before God and so cannot endure the rigors of God's standards.

> Howbeit we speak wisdom among them that are perfect: yet not the wisdom of this world, nor of the princes of this world, that come to nought: But we speak the wisdom of God in a mystery, even the hidden wisdom, which God ordained before the world unto our glory. (1 Corinthians 2:6–7)

> Where is the wise? where is the scribe? where is the disputer of this world? hath not God made foolish the wisdom of this world? For after that in the wisdom of God the world by wisdom knew not God, it pleased God by the foolishness of preaching to save them that believe. For the Jews require a sign, and the Greeks seek after wisdom: But we preach Christ crucified, unto the Jews a stumblingblock, and unto the Greeks foolishness; But unto them which are called, both Jews and Greeks, Christ the power of God, and the wisdom of God. Because the foolishness of God is wiser than men; and the weakness of God is stronger than men. (1 Corinthians 1:20–25)

As a result, the house of discipleship of our Christian life must be anchored on the divine, winning wisdom of God. Truly speaking, there is not much we can do without sticking closely to this heavenly wisdom. Solomon counseled that wisdom remained the main ingredient of a successful Christian, God-approved life and urged us to desperately reach out for it.

Get wisdom! Get understanding! Do not forget, nor turn away from the words of my mouth. Wisdom is the principal thing: therefore get wisdom, and in all your getting, get understanding. (Proverbs 4:5, 7)

Solomon caught this revelation as well.

Through wisdom is an house builded; and by understanding it is established: And by knowledge shall the chambers be filled with all precious and pleasant riches. (Proverbs 24:3–4)

God built and established the world with his supernatural wisdom and knowledge, so it stands to reason that if the church must effectively build and perfect the discipleship work God gave it, it needs to apply the wholesome, supernatural wisdom of God.

And Jesus came and spake unto them, saying, All power is given unto me in heaven and in earth. Go ye therefore, and teach all nations, baptizing them in the name of the Father, and of the Son, and of the Holy Ghost: Teaching them to observe all things whatsoever I have commanded you: and, lo, I am with you always, even unto the end of the world. Amen. (Matthew 28:18–20)

Jeremiah captured this revelation as well.

He hath made the earth by his power, he hath established the world by his wisdom, and hath stretched out the heaven by his understanding. (Jeremiah 51:15)

Friends, we must exercise the divine winning wisdom of God in our discipleship work by declaring the wholesome, undiluted word of God without adding to or subtracting from it. Jesus told us that only then can we lay claim to being true Christian disciples.

> Every word of God is pure: he is a shield unto them that put their trust in him. Add thou not unto his words, lest he reprove thee, and thou be found a liar. (Proverbs 30:5–6)

God also gave Moses this revelation when he was building the Old Testament discipleship structure for the children of Israel.

> Now therefore hearken, O Israel, unto the statutes and unto the judgments, which I teach you, for to do them, that ye may live, and go in and possess the land which the Lord God of your fathers giveth you. Ye shall not add unto the word which I command you, neither shall ye diminish ought from it, that ye may keep the commandments of the Lord your God which I command you. (Deuteronomy 4:1–2)

> What thing soever I command you, observe to do it: thou shalt not add thereto, nor diminish from it. (Deuteronomy 12:32)

With the spirit of wisdom, Jesus, Paul, and other New Testament apostles interacted with unbelievers and engrafted them into discipleship programs. Paul became all things to all men in a concerted effort to win some over to God. He never stopped asking fellow believers everywhere to pray and ask God to give him the spirit of wisdom and revelation.

> For if I do this thing willingly, I have a reward: but if against my will, a dispensation of the gospel is committed unto me. What is my reward then? Verily that, when I preach the gospel, I may make the gospel of Christ without charge, that I abuse not my power in the gospel. For though I be free from all men, yet have I made myself servant unto all, that I might gain the more. And unto the Jews I became as a Jew, that I might gain the Jews; to them that are under the law, as under the law, that I might gain them that are under the law; To them that are without law, as without law, (being not without law to God, but under the law to Christ,) that I might gain them that are without law. To the weak became I as weak, that I might gain the weak: I am made all things to all men, that I might by all means save some. And this I do for the gospel's sake, that I might be partaker thereof with you. (1 Corinthians 9:17–23)

The beloved apostle Paul, writing under the guidance of the Holy Spirit, enjoined us, the church of God, to grow in heavenly wisdom so our discipleship programs would be patterned according to the wisdom of the cross. Paul treasured the wisdom and knowledge of God that he pressed forward to reach out for more in-depth knowledge of God's revelation. He eventually succeeded in building a perfect, heaven-approved discipleship program for the Lord.

> For this cause we also, since the day we heard it, do not cease to pray for you, and to desire that ye might be filled with the knowledge of his will in all wisdom and spiritual understanding; That ye might walk worthy of the Lord unto all pleasing, being fruitful in every good work, and increasing in the knowledge of God; Strengthened with all might, according to his glorious power, unto all patience and longsuffering with joyfulness; Giving thanks unto the Father, which hath made us meet to be partakers of the inheritance of the saints in light: Who hath delivered us from the power of darkness, and hath translated us into the kingdom of his dear Son: Whom we preach, warning every man, and teaching every man in all wisdom; that we may present every man perfect in Christ Jesus. (Colossians 1:9–13, 28)

> For Christ sent me not to baptize, but to preach the gospel: not with wisdom of words, lest the cross of Christ should be made of none effect. (1 Corinthians 1:17)

We need to learn the mind of God by having the wisdom of Christ to start and finish the discipleship work given to the church by God. Jesus Christ is the express reflection of his heavenly Father and knows the ultimate intents, purposes, and will of God. He is the embodiment of the divine wisdom that accomplishes the divine purposes of God on earth. Jesus told us bluntly that without him we could do nothing.

> Abide in me, and I in you. As the branch cannot bear fruit of itself, except it abide in the vine; no more can ye, except ye abide in me. I am the vine, ye are the branches: He that abideth in me, and I in him, the same bringeth forth much fruit: for without me ye can do nothing. (John 15:4–5)

The church needs the fullness of Christ to accomplish God's purpose on earth. The church of God, which Jesus built over two thousand years ago in a tiny corner of the Middle East, is on an urgent earthly mission of reconciling a decadent, directionless world with our heavenly Father.

> But God hath revealed them unto us by his Spirit: for the Spirit searcheth all things, yea, the deep things of God. For what man knoweth the things of a man, save the spirit of man which is in him? Even so the things of God knoweth no man, but the Spirit of God. Now we have received, not the spirit of the world, but the spirit which is of God; that we might know the things that are freely given to us of God. Which things also we speak, not in the words which man's wisdom teacheth, but which the Holy Ghost teacheth; comparing spiritual things with

spiritual. But the natural man receiveth not the things of the Spirit of God: for they are foolishness unto him: neither can he know them, because they are spiritually discerned. But he that is spiritual judgeth all things, yet he himself is judged of no man. For who hath known the mind of the Lord, that he may instruct him? but we have the mind of Christ. (1 Corinthians 2:10–16)

In whom are hidden all the treasures of wisdom and knowledge. Now this I say lest anyone should deceive you with persuasive words. For though I am absent in the flesh, yet I am with you in spirit, rejoicing to see your *good* order and the steadfastness of your faith in Christ.

As you therefore have received Christ Jesus the Lord, so walk in Him, rooted and built up in Him and established in the faith, as you have been taught, abounding in it with thanksgiving.

Beware lest anyone cheat you through philosophy and empty deceit, according to the tradition of men, according to the basic principles of the world, and not according to Christ. For in Him dwells all the fullness of the Godhead bodily; and you are complete in Him, who is the head of all principality and power. (Colossians 2:3–10)

Grace

God's grace helps us in no small measure in building a heaven-approved discipleship structure. His grace represents the supernatural ability God gives individuals to accomplish divine tasks. It involves the unearned favor of God and, according to the *New Oxford Illustrated Dictionary*, "regenerating, inspiring, and strengthening influence" given by God to propel the church to construct the heaven-envisioned discipleship ark that accommodates those called by God to heaven. The apostle Paul and other servants of God recognized and treasured the great importance of God's grace in their Christian lives and ministries and prayed God to grant it to their followers.

> Unto the church of God which is at Corinth, to them that are sanctified in Christ Jesus, called to be saints, with all that in every place call upon the name of Jesus Christ our Lord, both theirs and ours: Grace be unto you, and peace, from God our Father, and from the Lord Jesus Christ. I thank my God always on your behalf, for the grace of God which is given you by Jesus Christ; That in every thing ye are enriched by him, in all utterance, and in all knowledge; Even as the testimony of Christ was confirmed in you: So that ye come behind in no gift; waiting for the coming of our Lord Jesus Christ: Who shall also confirm you unto the end, that ye may be blameless in the day of our Lord Jesus Christ. (1 Corinthians 1:2–8)

Even when we were dead in sins, hath quickened us together with Christ, (by grace ye are saved;)And hath raised us up together, and made us sit together in heavenly places in Christ Jesus: That in the ages to come he might shew the exceeding riches of his grace in his kindness toward us through Christ Jesus. For by grace are ye saved through faith; and that not of yourselves: it is the gift of God: In whom all the building fitly framed together groweth unto an holy temple in the Lord: In whom ye also are builded together for an habitation of God through the Spirit. (Ephesians 2:5–8, 21–22)

We need the strengthening and supportive influence of God's grace to effectively build strong, lasting, and heaven-approved discipleship. Paul, Peter, and other servants of God were all generously given this enabling grace, and they built a virile and lasting discipleship structure that stood the test of time. The current church dispensation is being enjoined by God to improve on the legacies of these faithful builders and messengers of God by drawing from the well of grace of God's glorious throne.

For we are labourers together with God: ye are God's husbandry, ye are God's building. According to the grace of God which is given unto me, as a wise masterbuilder, I have laid the foundation, and another buildeth thereon. But let every man take heed how he buildeth thereupon. For other foundation can no man lay than that is laid, which is Jesus Christ. (1 Corinthians 3:9–11)

The grace of God aptly defines the nature, size, and scope of our discipleship work and generates favor and divine approval. It is an essential ingredient intended by God to lubricate the wheels of discipleship to avoid a wreck.

> And when James, Cephas, and John, who seemed to be pillars, perceived the grace that was given unto me, they gave to me and Barnabas the right hands of fellowship; that we should go unto the heathen, and they unto the circumcision. Only they would that we should remember the poor; the same which I also was forward to do. (Galatians 2:9–10)

> But unto every one of us is given grace according to the measure of the gift of Christ. And he gave some, apostles; and some, prophets; and some, evangelists; and some, pastors and teachers; For the perfecting of the saints, for the work of the ministry, for the edifying of the body of Christ: Till we all come in the unity of the faith, and of the knowledge of the Son of God, unto a perfect man, unto the measure of the stature of the fulness of Christ. (Ephesians 4:7, 11–13)

It is also imperative to highlight one more important role divine grace plays in discipleship. The grace of God takes the church into the divine presence of God in order to obtain revelational insights or secrets of the knowledge and wisdom of God, and this enables it to effectively build and sustain the discipleship work given to it. Discipleship is a divine call or invitation to a covenant relationship with God, and as a consequence, it requires covenant secrets from heaven to make it work properly. The church, therefore must of necessity strive to enter God's throne of grace to receive these divine secrets.

> Let us therefore come boldly unto the throne of grace, that we may obtain mercy, and find grace to help in time of need. (Hebrews 4:16)

David strengthened this revelation when he wrote,

> The secret of the LORD is with them that fear him; and he will shew them his covenant. (Psalm 25:14)

The apostle Paul repositioned this revelation in this light.

> If ye have heard of the dispensation of the grace of God which is given me to you-ward: How that by revelation he made known unto me the mystery; (as I wrote afore in few words, Whereby, when ye read, ye may understand my knowledge in the mystery of Christ)Which in other ages was not made known unto the sons of men, as it is now revealed unto his holy apostles and prophets by the Spirit; That the Gentiles should be fellow heirs, and of the same body, and partakers of his promise in Christ by the gospel: Whereof I was made a minister, according to the gift of the grace of God given unto me by the effectual working of his power. Unto me, who am less than the least of all saints, is this grace given, that I should preach among the Gentiles the unsearchable

riches of Christ; And to make all men see what is the fellowship of the mystery, which from the beginning of the world hath been hid in God, who created all things by Jesus Christ: To the intent that now unto the principalities and powers in heavenly places might be known by the church the manifold wisdom of God. (Ephesians 3:2–10)

CHAPTER 9

The Role of Prayer in Discipleship

Praying always with all prayer and supplication in the
spirit, being watchful to this end with all perseverance and
supplication for all saints, and for me, that I may open my
mouth boldly to make known the mystery of the gospel.
—Ephesians 6:18–19

Prayer is needed for the bonding, unity, and consolidation of the
work of the discipleship of the church of God on earth. It helps oil
the wheels of the Great Commission. We can never wish away the
important and unique role prayer plays in the effective construction
and running of the great task of discipleship. Jesus enjoined his
disciples to ask God in prayer to grant them help in the harvest work
confronting them.

After these things the Lord appointed other seventy
also, and sent them two and two before his face into
every city and place, wither he himself would come.
Therefore said he unto them, the harvest is truly
great, but the laborers are few: pray ye therefore the

Lord of the harvest, that he will send forth labourers into his harvest. (Luke 10:1–2)

The harvest in this passage refers to the end-time apostolic discipleship work God expect his church on earth to effectively embark upon.

Jesus, Paul, and others prayed for and got his directions and support for the effective erection and completion of their discipleship programs. Jesus offered a prayer of sanctification for his disciples to his heavenly Father to enable them to bond perfectly.

These words spake Jesus, and lifted up his eyes to Heaven and said, Father, the hour has come: glorify thy son, that thy son may also glorify thee: I pray for them: I pray not for the world, but for them which thou has given me; for they are thine. I pray not that thou shouldest take them out of the world, but that thou shouldest keep them from evil. Neither pray I for these alone, but for them also, which shall believe on me through their word; that they all may be one: as thou, Father, art in me, and I in thee, that they also may be one in us: that the world may believe that thou has sent me. (John 17:1–9, 15, 20, 21)

Jesus never underscored the unique importance of the prayer ministry during his earthly discipleship work. He consistently prayed to his heavenly Father to assist his discipleship work with revelation, strength, and direction. He often separated himself from his disciples and withdrew to a mountain or a seaside to spend quality time praying, meditating, and receiving further instructions, directions, power, and revelations from God, who had sent him to build and perfect the discipleship work of the church. Jesus passed on this art of prayer to his disciples to enable them to be successful in their discipleship programs. He commanded them to pray constantly and never underestimate the power of the prayer ministry.

> Immediately Jesus made his disciple get into the boat and go before him to the other side, while he sent the multitude away: And when he had sent the multitude away, he went up on the mountain by himself to pray. Now when evening came, he was alone there. (Matthew 14:22–23)

> So He himself often withdrew into the wilderness and prayed. Now it happen on a certain day, as he was teaching, that there were Pharisees and teachers of the law sitting by, who had come out of every town of Galilee, Judea and Jerusalem. And the power of the Lord was present to heal them. (Luke 5:16–17; see also Mark 6:45–46; Matthew 26:36; Luke 18:1)

Jesus reminded Peter that he has prayed for him for strength and commanded him to also pray and strengthen the disciples he had committed to his care and leadership when he was delivered and established in the power of God. In Matthew 6, Jesus showed the divine pattern of prayer that would help his church establish the discipleship program of God's kingdom on earth. He commanded them to seek and crave for the establishment and effective running of God's discipleship work on earth first as precondition for the unimpeded release of God's divine abundance.

> In this manner, therefore, pray: our Father in Heaven,
> hallowed be your name, your kingdom come, your
> will be done on earth as it is in Heaven, give us
> this day our daily bread and forgive us our debts,
> as we forgive our debtors. And do not lead us into
> temptation. But deliver us from the evil one. For
> yours is the kingdom and the power and the glory
> forever Amen. But seek first the kingdom of God and
> his righteousness and all these things shall be added
> unto you. (Matthew 6:9–13, 33)

Prayer enables the church of Christ to discover the perfect will of God necessary for the construction and completion of His discipleship programs. The perfect will of God releases the divine wisdom we need to building on the solid apostolic foundations Jesus laid when he built his church and when he walked the streets of this confused, directionless world. The apostle James advised the church to pray for God's wisdom to enable it build effectively.

> If any of you lack wisdom, let him ask of God, that
> giveth to all men liberally, and upbraideth not; and it
> shall be given him. But let him ask in faith, nothing
> wavering. For he that wavereth is like a wave of the
> sea driven with the wind and tossed. For let not that
> man think that he shall receive any thing of the Lord.
> A double minded man is unstable in all his ways.
> (James 1:5–8)

Without discovering the perfect will of God in prayer, the church is in danger of building discipleship structures that will not stand the rigors of God's standards. Jesus sought and walked in the perfect will of God and effectively finished the work of discipleship God had given him.

> Then they came to a place which was named Gethsemane: and he said to his disciples, sit here while I pray: then he said to them, my soul is exceedingly sorrowful, even to death. Stay here and watch. He went a little further and fell on the ground and prayed that if it were possible, the hour might pass from him. And he said, Abba Father, all things are possible for you. Take this cup away from me: nevertheless, not what I will but what you will. (Mark 14:32, 34, 36)

The apostle Paul stated this revelation in this light.

> Therefore I also, after I heard of your faith in the Lord Jesus and your love for all the saints, do not cease to give thanks for you, making mention of you in my prayers: that the God of our Lord Jesus Christ, the Father of glory, may give to you the Spirit of wisdom and revelation in the knowledge of Him ... which is his body, the fullness of him who fills all in all. (Ephesians 1:17–19, 23)

Healing, deliverance, and miracles are the noticeable features of effective heaven-approved discipleship that attracts a confused, sick, and directionless world to the loving arm of a waiting God. Prayer makes easily available the yoke-destroying anointing of this loving and caring God to abound in discipleship. The Scriptures recorded that God anointed Jesus and, by implication, his messengers to heal and set captives free. These servants of God released this divine power through the instrument of prayer. With effective prayer, we can touch the gracious and saving arms of God to heal and draw multitudes of men and women into his divine kingdom.

> And when he has sent them away, he departed to the mountain to pray: and when they came out of the boat immediately the people, recognised him; Ran through that whole surrounding region, and began to carry about on their beds those who were sick to wherever they heard he was: wherever he entered, into villages, cities, or the country, they laid the sick in the market place, and begged him that they might just touch the hem of his garment. And as many as touched him were made well. (Mark 6:46, 54–56)

The apostles and disciples of the first apostolic era fervently sought God in consistent prayer sessions, and they were used greatly in healing, delivering, and discipling numerous people into God's discipleship programs. They carried on with this ministry of prayer Jesus handed to them.

> And they continued steadfastly in the apostles' doctrine and fellowship [discipleship] in the breaking of bread and prayers. Then fear came upon every soul, and many wonders and signs were done through the apostles: praising God and having favor with all people. And the Lord added to the church those who were being saved. (Acts 2:42–43, 47)

Now Peter and John went up together to the temple at the hour of prayer, the ninth hour. And a certain man lame from his mother's womb was carried, whom they laid daily at the gate of the temple which was called beautiful, to ask alms from those who entered the temple; who seeing Peter and John about to go into the temple, asked for arms: and fixing his eyes on him with John, Peter said, look at us: so he gave them his attention, expecting to receive something from them. then Peter said, silver and gold I do not have but what I have I give you: in the name of Jesus Christ of Nazareth, rise up and walk: and he took him by the right hand and Lifted him up, and immediately his feet and ankle bones received strength: And all the people saw him walking and praising God. (Acts 3:1–8, 9)

It is imperative to stress that Peter, the head of the disciples, realized this and devised a way to stick to the ministry of prayer and the Word, and he delegated the other arms of leadership of the church to others to avoid distractions that would obstruct the release of God's power required to finish the discipleship work. He placed great importance on the prayer ministry and prospered tremendously.

Now in those days, when the number of the disciples was multiplying, there arose a complaint against the Hebrews by the Hellenists, because their widows were neglected in the daily distribution: then the twelve summoned the multitude of disciples and said, it is not desirable that we should leave the word of God and serve tables: therefore, brethren seek out from among you seven men of good reputation, full of the Holy Spirit and wisdom, who we may appoint over this business; but we will give ourselves continually to prayer and to the ministry of the word. Then the word of God spread and the number of disciples multiplied greatly in Jerusalem, and a great many of the priests were obedient to the faith. (Acts 6:1–4, 7)

Prayer helps build and sustain the discipleship work of the church. When the church was being persecuted in its formative stages, the disciples used prayer to survive. God came down and released his power to protect and sustain the church and its wheels of discipleship. Peter, Paul, and Silas were all delivered by the mighty power of God through the instrument of prayer.

Now about that time Herod the king stretched forth his hands to vex certain of the church. And he killed James the brother of John with the sword. And because he saw it pleased the Jews, he proceeded further to take Peter also. (Then were the days of unleavened bread.) And when he had apprehended him, he put him in prison, and delivered him to four quaternions of soldiers to keep him; intending after Easter to bring him forth to the people. Peter therefore was kept in prison: but prayer was made without ceasing of the church unto God for him. And when Herod would have brought him forth, the same night Peter was sleeping between two soldiers, bound with two chains: and the keepers before the door kept the prison. And, behold, the angel of the Lord came upon him, and a light shined in the prison: and he smote Peter on the side, and raised him up, saying, Arise up quickly. And his chains fell off from his hands. And the angel said unto him, Gird thyself, and bind on thy sandals. And so he did. And he saith unto him, Cast thy garment about thee, and follow me. And he went out, and followed him; and wist not that it was true which was done by the angel; but thought he saw a vision. When they were past the first and the second ward, they came unto the iron gate that leadeth unto the city; which opened to them of his own accord: and they went out, and passed on through one street; and forthwith the angel departed from him. And when Peter was come to himself, he said, Now I know of a surety, that the Lord hath sent his angel, and hath delivered me out of the hand of Herod, and from all the expectation of the people of the Jews. And when he had considered the thing, he came to the house of Mary the mother of John, whose surname was Mark; where many were gathered together praying. And as Peter knocked at the door of the gate, a damsel came to hearken, named Rhoda. And when she knew Peter's voice, she opened not the gate for gladness, but ran in, and told how Peter stood before the gate. And they said unto her, Thou art mad. But she constantly affirmed that it was even so. Then said they, It is his angel. But Peter continued knocking: and when they had opened the door, and saw him, they were astonished.

But he, beckoning unto them with the hand to hold their peace, declared unto them how the Lord had brought him out of the prison. And he said, Go shew these things unto James, and to the brethren. And he departed, and went into another place. Now as soon as it was day, there was no small stir among the soldiers, what was become of Peter. And when Herod had sought for him, and found him not, he examined the keepers, and commanded that they should be put to death. And he went down from Judaea to Caesarea, and there abode. And Herod was highly displeased with them of Tyre and Sidon: but they came with one accord to him, and, having made Blastus the king's chamberlain their friend, desired peace; because their country was nourished by the king's country. (Acts 12:1–20)

And the multitude rose up together against them: and the magistrates rent off their clothes, and commanded to beat them. And when they had laid many stripes upon them, they cast them into prison, charging the jailor to keep them safely: Who, having received such a charge, thrust them into the inner prison, and made their feet fast in the stocks. And at midnight Paul and Silas prayed, and sang praises unto God: and the prisoners heard them. And suddenly there was a great earthquake, so that the foundations of the prison were shaken: and immediately all the doors were opened, and every one's bands were loosed. And the keeper of the prison awaking out of his sleep, and seeing the prison doors open, he drew out his sword, and would have killed himself, supposing that the prisoners had been fled. But Paul cried with a loud voice, saying, Do thyself no harm: for we are all here. Then he called for a light, and sprang in, and came trembling, and fell down before Paul and Silas, And brought them out, and said, Sirs, what must I do to be saved? And they said, Believe on the Lord Jesus Christ, and thou shalt be saved, and thy house. And they spake unto him the word of the Lord, and to all that were in his house. And he took them the same hour of the night, and washed their stripes; and was baptized, he and all his, straightway. (Acts 16:22–30, 31–33)

The role of prayer in the discipleship work of the church can never be wished away. Prayer plays a strategic role and defines the life, size, and quality of discipleship in the church. It generates and sustains the divine power to build. The greater the amount of prayer, the greater the power generated, and as a consequence, the clearer and better the size and quality of our discipleship work offered to the Lord.

CHAPTER 10

Discipleship and Quality Control

Not everyone who says Lord, Lord shall enter the Kingdom of
Heaven, but He who does the will of my Father in Heaven.
—Matthew 7:21

I begin the final chapter of this book by defining two key words,
control and *quality*. The *New Oxford Illustrated Dictionary* defines
control as the "function or power of directing and regulating." It
equally means to "restrain, check or standard of comparison for
checking inferences from experiment, etc." The same dictionary
defines *quality* as the "degree of excellence, relative nature or kind
or character: class or grade of thing as determined by this, general
excellence."

In some professional organizations, supervisory bodies regulate the
professional works or activities of their rank and file. In the publishing
industry, for instance, a body assigns ISBNs (international standard
book number) to help regulate the publications and distribution of
high-quality books, magazines, and such. This is equally true in the
food and beverages industries and other manufacturing concerns in
which similar bodies with the same regulatory functions exist. God

expects us to put our Christian ministry or discipleship to effective and qualitative use.

> And the foolish said unto the wise, Give us of your oil; for our lamps are gone out. But the wise answered, saying, Not so; lest there be not enough for us and you: but go ye rather to them that sell, and buy for yourselves. And while they went to buy, the bridegroom came; and they that were ready went in with him to the marriage: and the door was shut. Afterward came also the other virgins, saying, Lord, Lord, open to us. But he answered and said, Verily I say unto you, I know you not. Watch therefore, for ye know neither the day nor the hour wherein the Son of man cometh. For the kingdom of heaven is as a man travelling into a far country, who called his own servants, and delivered unto them his goods. (Matthew 25:8–14)

I believe strongly that God, for this reason, has a spiritual regulatory body, the Holy Spirit, to assign spiritual ISBNs to every aspect of the discipleship program of the church to help check the spiritual and physical decay of the church. Every human life is a book written and directed by God.

> And I saw the dead, small and great, stand before God; and the books were opened: and another book was opened, which is the book of life: and the dead were judged out of those things which were written in the books, according to their works. And whosoever was

not found written in the book of life was cast into the
lake of fire. (Revelation 20:12, 15)

Friends, before true discipleship can be fully constructed, God must
conform us to the image of his Son. He knows when our discipleship
works are acceptable to him and speaks through the leadership of the
church for amendment.

> And we know that all things work together for good
> to those who love God, to those who are the called
> according to his purpose: For whom He foreknew,
> He also predestined to be conformed to the image
> of his son, that he might be the first born of the
> brethren. (Romans 8:28–29)

> Then Haggai answered and said, so is these people
> and so is this nation before me, says the Lord, and so
> is every work of their hands: and what they offer there
> is unclean. (Haggai 1:14)

God uses the ministry of the Holy Spirit as a quality control measure
to arrest spiritual decline and thus regulate the quality of discipleship
in the whole of the church. The leadership must be spiritually
sensitive, visionary, and spiritually and physically disciplined, and
it must, without fail, inject these laudable qualities into the lives of
all church members. They must be given wholly to total holiness
and purity of life, since discipleship is a solid platform for spiritual
progression. Quality control will enable the church to build an
enduring fellowship with God.

The teachings Jesus gave during his earthly ministry, together with the Holy Spirit, inspired the Pauline and other epistles. They were intended to instill the highest quality of heaven-approved discipleship in the church.

Friends, the church cannot claim to maintain the purity and standards of God's holiness, its foundation, if it continues to be polluted by the fashions and systems of this wicked and passing world. There must be a controlled separation from the world and a distinction drawn between the church and the world. The apostle John presented this revelation thus.

> Do not love the world or the things in the world. If anyone loves the world, the love of the Father is not in him: for all that it is in the world, the lust of the flesh, the lust of the eyes, and the pride of life, is not of the Father but of the world. And the world is passing away, and the lust of it, but he who does the will of God abides forever. (1 John 2:15–17)

James repositioned this revealed truth when he wrote,

> You ask and do not receive because you ask amiss that you may spend it on your pleasures. Adulterers and adulteresses! Do you not know that friendship with the world is enmity with God? Whoever, therefore wants to be a friend of the world makes himself an enemy of God. (James 4:3–4)

The church needs to learn and walk in the true doctrines of our Lord Jesus Christ with full concentration so it can walk in the divine light the Word generates.

> In him was life, and the life was the light of men;
> that was the true light which gives life to everyone
> coming into the world. (John 1:4, 9)

Communication plays an important role in sustaining the quality of discipleship in the church. The Christian believers at Berea were more spiritually mature as a result of a well-defined communication network with the Word of God and the teachings of the apostle Paul. The earliest apostolic churches maintained quality-controlled discipleship because of good communication networks among themselves. They faithfully communicated the Word of God with measured humility and clarity. God wants the wholesome message of his Word correctly and fully communicated to a confused and directionless world so he can reconcile humanity to himself.

> Then the brethren immediately sent Paul and Silas away by night to Berea. When they arrived, they went into the Synagogue of the Jews. These were more fair-minded than those in Thessalonica, in that they received the word with all readiness, and searched the scriptures daily to find out whether those things were so: therefore many of them believeth, and also not a few of the Greeks, prominent women as well as men. (Acts 17:10–12; see also 2 Peter 1:10–13; 2 Timothy 2:15)

Friends, I pray that God will destroy and remove every trace of darkness from his church as its members humble themselves and leaf through the Scriptures, in Jesus' name, amen.

In a true discipleship structure, God expects the church's members to put off the garment of sin and worldliness and replace it with the garments of salvation, holiness, and purity of life. This is where the twin concepts of character and integrity come in. Character and integrity sustain the anointing God has released on the church for the work of discipleship. What determines, and by implication, approves our discipleship work by God is the character of the Spirit of God, as Paul wrote.

> But the fruit of the Spirit is love, joy, peace, longsuffering, kindness, goodness, faithfulness, gentleness, self-control. Against such there is no law. And those who are Christ's have crucified the flesh with its passions and desires. (Galatians 5:22–24)

The church must distance itself from the dangerous, liberal theological viewpoint of once saved, always saved. It hurts and slows the wheels of discipleship of the church and pollutes the purity and quality of discipleship. The grace of God has washed and saved us—the church—and has equally given us a responsibility that is unique and distinct from the world of sin.

> For the grace of God that brings salvation has appeared to all men; teachings us that, denying ungodly and worldly lusts, we should live soberly, righteously and godly in the present age, looking for the blessed

hope and glorious appearing of our great God and Savior, Jesus Christ, who gave himself for us, that he might redeem us from every lawless deed and purify for himself his own special people, zealous for good works. (Titus 2:11–14)

The church has unfortunately boxed the Holy Spirit—the regulatory authority—into a tight corner and has opened its doors to Satan and his world to ruin the discipleship work the priceless blood of our Lord Jesus Christ started. The foundations of holiness, purity, and complete obedience, upon which the church of God has been built, are gradually being destroyed, and the serpent is seriously biting off the foundational structures of the church.

It is very bad and sounds inexplicable, for instance, that homosexuality—a societal problem—and other vices the church has attempted to provide solutions for by means of biblical approaches have been allowed to wreck the foundations of the church.

The acceptance and ordination of homosexuals and the emergence and recognition of gay and lesbian human-rights communities in the church has done great damage to it. This immoral trend has seriously demeaned and decreased the quality and purity of discipleship, and it must be stopped.

Do you not know that the unrighteous will not inherit the kingdom of God? Do not be deceived. Neither fornicators, nor idolaters, nor adulterers, nor homosexuals, nor sodomites, nor thieves, nor covetous, nor drunkards, nor revilers, nor extortioners will inherit the kingdom of God. And such were some of you. But you were washed, but you were sanctified, but you were justified in the name of the Lord Jesus and by the Spirit of our God.

Do you not know that your bodies are members of Christ? Shall I then take the members of Christ and make them members of a harlot? Certainly not!

Flee sexual immorality. Every sin that a man does is outside the body, but he who commits sexual immorality sins against his own body. Or do you not know that your body is the temple of the Holy Spirit who is in you, whom you have from God, and you are not your own? For you were bought at a price; therefore glorify God in your body and in your spirit, which are God's. (1 Corinthians 6:9–11, 15, 18–20)

Therefore God also gave them up to uncleanness, in the lusts of their hearts, to dishonor their bodies among themselves, who exchanged the truth of God for the lie, and worshiped and served the creature rather than the Creator, who is blessed forever. Amen. For this reason God gave them up to vile passions. For even their women exchanged the natural use for what is against nature. Likewise also the men, leaving the natural use of the woman, burned in their lust for one another, men with men committing what is shameful, and receiving in themselves the penalty of their error which was due. And even as they did not like to retain God in their knowledge, God gave them over to a debased mind, to do those things which are not fitting; being filled with all unrighteousness, sexual immorality, wickedness, covetousness, maliciousness; full of envy, murder, strife, deceit, evil-mindedness; they are whisperers, backbiters, haters of God, violent, proud, boasters, inventors of evil things, disobedient to parents, undiscerning, untrustworthy, unloving, unforgiving, unmerciful; who, knowing the righteous judgment of God, that those who practice such things are deserving of death, not only do the same but also approve of those who practice them. (Romans 1:24–32)

For fornicators, for sodomites, for kidnappers, for liars, for perjurers, and if there is any other thing that is contrary to sound doctrine, according to the glorious gospel of the blessed God which was committed to my trust. (1 Timothy 1:10–11)

We need to ask, are the multitudes in our churches real? We can observe the sudden rise of counterfeit Christianity or discipleship in this current dispensation just as Jesus predicted in Matthew 24 and as was noticed in the days of the prophet Jeremiah. Jesus predicted that in the end time, two conflicting Christian groups would emerge: the Christian church group he founded and that would be led by the Holy Spirit, which would be faithful to his teachings, and the other group, which would be led and influenced by a deceitful Spirit. This group would accept the name of Christ but deny him in works and distort his doctrinal teachings and, as a consequence, create a distorted discipleship model of the church God purchased with the precious blood of his Son.

> Then I saw another beast coming up out of the earth, and he had two horns like a lamb and spoke like a dragon. And he exercises all the authority of the first beast in his presence, and causes the earth and those who dwell in it to worship the first beast, whose deadly wound was healed. He performs great signs, so that he even makes fire come down from heaven on the earth in the sight of men. And he deceives those who dwell on the earth by those signs which he was granted to do in the sight of the beast, telling those who dwell on the earth to make an image to the beast who was wounded by the sword and lived. (Revelation 13:11–14)

The apostle Paul described this Christian group.

> But what I do, I will also continue to do, that I may cut off the opportunity from those who desire an opportunity to be regarded just as we are in the things of which they boast. For such are false apostles, deceitful workers, transforming themselves into apostles of Christ. And no wonder! For Satan himself transforms himself into an angel of light. Therefore it is no great thing if his ministers also transform themselves into ministers of righteousness, whose end will be according to their works. (1 Corinthians 11:12–15)

This opposing group of Christian believers will stop at nothing to distort the doctrine of God, ranging from the laws of God and the grace of salvation to living the life of purity and holiness God has commanded. Lawlessness remains the key element of the diluted message of these false teachers and messengers, and this makes it appealing and attractive.

Friends, disregard or contempt for God's laws and grace will form the foundation of this supposedly successful and popular but false discipleship. However, Jesus rejects such teachers with their doctrines of lawlessness and distorted view of the grace of God. In Matthew 7, Jesus showed his grave opposition and condemnation of such false messengers with their counterfeit revival fire.

> Not everyone who says to Me, "Lord, Lord," shall enter the kingdom of heaven, but he who does the will of My Father in heaven. Many will say to Me in that day, "Lord, Lord, have we not prophesied in Your name, cast out demons in Your name, and done many wonders in Your name?" And then I will declare to them, "I never knew you; depart from Me, you who practice lawlessness!" (Matthew 7:21–23)

> Then the scribes and Pharisees who were from Jerusalem came to Jesus, saying, "Why do Your disciples transgress the tradition of the elders? For they do not wash their hands when they eat bread." He answered and said to them, "Why do you also transgress the commandment of God because of your tradition? For God commanded, saying, 'Honor your

father and your mother'; and, 'He who curses father or mother, let him be put to death.' But you say, 'Whoever says to his father or mother, "Whatever profit you might have received from me is a gift to God"— then he need not honor his father or mother.' Thus you have made the commandment of God of no effect by your tradition. Hypocrites! Well did Isaiah prophesy about you, saying: 'These people draw near to Me with their mouth, And honor Me with their lips, But their heart is far from Me. And in vain they worship Me, Teaching as doctrines the commandments of men.'" (Matthew 15:1–9)

For laying aside the commandment of God, ye hold the tradition of men, as the washing of pots and cups: and many other such like things ye do. And he said unto them, Full well ye reject the commandment of God, that ye may keep your own tradition. (Mark 7:8–9)

The church of God, though universal in nature, shape, and structure, is made up of various units that must all retain and reflect the nature and structure of the main church's discipleship structure. They must all speak with one voice. The prophet Zephaniah aptly captured this revelation when he wrote,

For then I will restore to the peoples a pure language, that they all may call on the name of the Lord, to serve Him with one accord; from beyond the rivers of Ethiopia. My worshipers, the daughter of my dispersed ones, shall bring my offering; in that day you shall not be shamed for any of your deeds in which you transgress against me. For then I will take away from your midst, those who rejoice in your pride, and you shall no longer be haughty in my holy mountain. The remnant of Israel shall do no unrighteousness and speak no lies, nor shall a deceitful tongue be found in their mouth; for they shall feed their flocks and lie down, and no one shall make them afraid. (Zephaniah 3:9–11, 13)

For as the body is one, and hath many members, and all the members of that one body, being many, are one body: so also is Christ. For by one Spirit are we all baptized into one body, whether we be Jews or Gentiles, whether we be bond or free; and have been all made to drink into one Spirit. For the body is not one member, but many. (1 Corinthians 12:12–14)

And in their mouth was found no guile: for they are without fault before the throne of God. And I saw another angel fly in the midst of heaven, having the everlasting gospel to preach unto them that dwell on the earth, and to every nation, and kindred, and tongue, and people. saying with a loud voice, Fear God, and give glory to him; for the hour of his judgment is come: and worship him that made heaven, and earth, and the sea, and the fountains of waters. (Revelation 14:5–7)

We urgently need to repent by retracing our steps and allowing the Holy Spirit to rebuild the fallen tabernacle, the discipleship structure of the church. God is reconstructing a new end-time apostolic discipleship ark that will propel his chosen people into heaven through the murky waters of this wicked, directionless world. He is raising his end-time army and equipping, supporting, and releasing them into this reconstruction work of his church on earth.

> On that day I will raise up the tabernacle of David, which has fallen down, and repair its damages; I will raise up its ruins, and rebuild it as in the days of old. (Amos 9:11)

The church Jesus built is supposed to be a light to the world of darkness. God commissioned the church to live a life of programmed scriptural, spiritual, and moral discipline and to point a decaying and directionless world toward the blazing path of this light of salvation and reformation. Our lives as true Christian believers is the mirror Jesus sends to this world of evil to transform lives. Jesus commands us to beam this light of salvation in us into the lives and shattered destinies of men and women trapped in the darkness enveloping the world.

> You are the light of the world. A city that is set on a hill cannot be hidden. Nor do they light a lamp and put it under a basket, but on a lampstand, and it gives light to all who are in the house. Let your light so shine before men, that they may see your good works and glorify your Father in heaven. (Matthew 5:14–16)

God is exposing the way of purity of life to the world through his tranformative agent, the church, just as he sent Jesus to mirror the image of God to the world that is in dire need of acceptable morality and purity of life. He therefore expects the discipleship structures of the church to measure up to his standards. God commanded Isaiah to set up a standard of purity of life for his people. God does not and would never lower his standards of expectation.

> Go through, go through the gates; prepare ye the way of the people; cast up, cast up the highway; gather out the stones; lift up a standard for the people. (Isaiah 62:10)

The apostle Peter encouraged the church membership as a matter of scriptural command to dutifully desire and work in true holiness and purity of life. Holiness and purity of life remain the true marks of genuine discipleship without which no one will see the Lord.

> But ye are a chosen generation, a royal priesthood, an holy nation, a peculiar people; that ye should shew forth the praises of him who hath called you out of darkness into his marvellous light; Dearly beloved, I beseech you as strangers and pilgrims, abstain from fleshly lusts, which war against the soul; Having your conversation honest among the Gentiles: that, whereas they speak against you as evildoers, they may by your good works, which they shall behold, glorify God in the day of visitation. (1 Peter 2:9, 11–12)

> Who gave himself for us, that he might redeem us from all iniquity, and purify unto himself a peculiar

people, zealous of good works. These things speak, and exhort, and rebuke with all authority. Let no man despise thee. (Titus 2:14–15)

This is a faithful saying, and these things I will that thou affirm constantly, that they which have believed in God might be careful to maintain good works. These things are good and profitable unto men. (Titus 3:8)

Follow peace with all men, and holiness, without which no man shall see the Lord. (Hebrews 12:14)

This is the law of the house; Upon the top of the mountain the whole limit thereof round about shall be most holy. Behold, this is the law of the house. ()

Having therefore these promises, dearly beloved, let us cleanse ourselves from all filthiness of the flesh and spirit, perfecting holiness in the fear of God. (2 Corinthians 7:1)

In that day shall there be upon the bells of the horses, Holiness Unto The Lord; and the pots in the Lord's house shall be like the bowls before the altar. Yea, every pot in Jerusalem and in Judah shall be holiness unto the Lord of hosts: and all they that sacrifice shall come and take of them, and seethe therein: and in that day there shall be no more the Canaanite in the house of the Lord of hosts. (Zachariah 14:20–21)

And every man that hath this hope in him purifieth himself, even as he is pure. Whosoever is born of God doth not commit sin; for his seed remaineth in him: and he cannot sin, because he is born of God. In this the children of God are manifest, and the children of the devil: whosoever doeth not righteousness is not of God, neither he that loveth not his brother. (1 John 3:3, 9–10)

For this is the will of God, even your sanctification, that ye should abstain from fornication: That every one of you should know how to possess his vessel in sanctification and honour. For God hath not called us unto uncleanness, but unto holiness. (1 Thessalonians 4:3–4, 7)

God uses the prophetic and teaching ministries of the church to sustain the quality and standards of discipleship in the church. Feeding and tending the flock, the disciples of God must never be underrated; it is the force that drives the wheels of discipleship and thus maintains its purity and quality. Jesus made this point clear.

Now ye are clean through the word which I have spoken unto you. (John 15:3)

Then shall I not be ashamed, when I have respect unto all thy commandments. Thy word have I hid in mine heart, that I might not sin against thee. (Psalm 119:9, 11)

Then will I sprinkle clean water upon you, and ye shall be clean: from all your filthiness, and from all your idols, will I cleanse you. A new heart also will I give you, and a new spirit will I put within you: and I will take away the stony heart out of your flesh, and I will give you an heart of flesh. (Ezekiel 36:25–26)

Sanctify them through thy truth: thy word is truth. (John 17:17)

The Word of faith we preach and teach and the Word of prophecy illuminate the inner part of the human heart and thus cleanse and lead it to spiritual progression and maturity in discipleship. Peter captured this revelation aptly when he wrote,

As newborn babes, desire the sincere milk of the word, that ye may grow thereby. (1 Peter 2:2)

And this voice which came from heaven we heard, when we were with him in the holy mount. We have also a more sure word of prophecy; whereunto ye do well that ye take heed, as unto a light that shineth in a dark place, until the day dawn, and the day star arise in your hearts: Knowing this first, that no prophecy of the scripture is of any private interpretation. For the prophecy came not in old time by the will of man: but holy men of God spake as they were moved by the Holy Ghost. (2 Peter 1:18–21)

Prophecy edifies and strengthens our Christian faith and walk with God. It drives the discipleship wheels of the church toward true Christian maturity, and as a consequence, it sustains the quality God demands in Christian fellowship. Paul noted the strengthening effects of prophecy.

> But he that prophesieth speaketh unto men to edification, and exhortation, and comfort. He that speaketh in an unknown tongue edifieth himself; but he that prophesieth edifieth the church. For ye may all prophesy one by one, that all may learn, and all may be comforted. (1 Corinthians 14:3–4, 31)

Friends, the main function of the teaching ministry is to build, warn, and encourage the disciples of Christ and to sustain the doctrinal teachings Jesus handed to the church. That explains why he commanded Peter, after the resurrection, to feed his disciples with the Word of God and reaffirmed that command when he gave them the kingdom work of the Great Commission.

> Go ye therefore, and teach all nations, baptizing them in the name of the Father, and of the Son, and of the Holy Ghost: Teaching them to observe all things whatsoever I have commanded you: and, lo, I am with you always, even unto the end of the world. Amen. (Matthew 28:19–20)

> He saith unto him the third time, Simon, son of Jonas, lovest thou me? Peter was grieved because he said unto him the third time, Lovest thou me? And

he said unto him, Lord, thou knowest all things; thou knowest that I love thee. Jesus saith unto him, Feed my sheep. (John 21:17)

God commanded Joshua to give undivided attention to the ministry of the Word and to strive at all costs to teach the children of Israel if he wanted to be successful in the discipleship program God gave to him. He subsequently became addicted to the Word and completed a successful discipleship program for God.

This book of the law shall not depart out of thy mouth; but thou shalt meditate therein day and night, that thou mayest observe to do according to all that is written therein: for then thou shalt make thy way prosperous, and then thou shalt have good success. (Joshua 1:8)

And Israel served the LORD all the days of Joshua, and all the days of the elders that overlived Joshua, and which had known all the works of the LORD, that he had done for Israel. (Joshua 24:31)

It was also through the instrument of prophecy and the teaching ministry of the Word that God enabled Jeremiah, Isaiah, and the apostles to change the unholy worship of the children of Israel and the Gentile nations to which their discipleship programs were exported. They were able to influence, change, and convert some reasonable numbers of lives into the kingdom of God and as a result built successful discipleship programs for the Lord.

> But we will give ourselves continually to prayer, and to the ministry of the word. And the word of God increased; and the number of the disciples multiplied in Jerusalem greatly; and a great company of the priests were obedient to the faith. (Acts 6:4, 7)

With the dramatic rise of counterfeit revival as a direct consequence of the construction of false discipleship structures, the church must strive for quality and purity of life. The church is a unique people chosen by God to receive eternal life. God expects the church to live a separated and holy life distinct from that of the world. Its members should, however, with God's wisdom and directions, engage the world and attempt to win it over to God. In doing so, God will approve our discipleship and guarantee us eternal and a blissful life in heaven.

> But ye are a chosen generation, a royal priesthood, an holy nation, a peculiar people; that ye should shew forth the praises of him who hath called you out of darkness into his marvellous light; Which in time past were not a people, but are now the people of God: which had not obtained mercy, but now have obtained mercy. Having your conversation honest among the Gentiles: that, whereas they speak against you as evildoers, they may by your good works, which they shall behold, glorify God in the day of visitation. (1 Peter 2:9–10, 12)

Biblical Passages for Further Reading

1. "For the children being not yet born, neither having done any good or evil, that the purpose of God according to election might stand, not of works, but of him that calleth; It was said unto her, The elder shall serve the younger. So then it is not of him that willeth, nor of him that runneth, but of God that sheweth mercy." Romans 9:11–12, 16

2. "As he saith also in Osee, I will call them my people, which were not my people; and her beloved, which was not beloved. And it shall come to pass, that in the place where it was said unto them, Ye are not my people; there shall they be called the children of the living God." Romans 9:25–26

3. "And when the king came in to see the guests, he saw there a man which had not on a wedding garment: And he saith unto him, Friend, how camest thou in hither not having a wedding garment? And he was speechless. Then said the king to the servants, Bind him hand and foot, and take him away, and cast him into outer darkness, there shall be weeping and gnashing of teeth. For many are called, but few are chosen." Matthew 22:11–14

4. "And have put on the new man, which is renewed in knowledge after the image of him that created him." Colossians 3:10

5. "I beseech you therefore, brethren, by the mercies of God, that ye present your bodies a living sacrifice, holy, acceptable unto God, which is your reasonable service. And be not conformed to this world: but be ye transformed by the renewing of your mind,

that ye may prove what is that good, and acceptable, and perfect, will of God." Romans 12:1–2

6. "For whom he did foreknow, he also did predestinate to be conformed to the image of his Son, that he might be the firstborn among many brethren." Romans 8:29

7. "Moreover whom he did predestinate, them he also called: and whom he called, them he also justified: and whom he justified, them he also glorified." Romans 8:30

8. " For we are his workmanship, created in Christ Jesus unto good works, which God hath before ordained that we should walk in them." Ephesians 2:10

9. "Wherefore remember, that ye being in time past Gentiles in the flesh, who are called Uncircumcision by that which is called the Circumcision in the flesh made by hands; That at that time ye were without Christ, being aliens from the commonwealth of Israel, and strangers from the covenants of promise, having no hope, and without God in the world: But now in Christ Jesus ye who sometimes were far off are made nigh by the blood of Christ." Ephesians 2:11–13

10. "And wisdom and knowledge shall be the stability of thy times, and strength of salvation: the fear of the LORD is his treasure." Isaiah 33:6

11. "Now therefore ye are no more strangers and foreigners, but fellowcitizens with the saints, and of the household of God; And

are built upon the foundation of the apostles and prophets, Jesus Christ himself being the chief corner stone; In whom all the building fitly framed together groweth unto an holy temple in the Lord: In whom ye also are builded together for an habitation of God through the Spirit." Ephesians 2:19–22

12. "I the LORD have called thee in righteousness, and will hold thine hand, and will keep thee, and give thee for a covenant of the people, for a light of the Gentiles; To open the blind eyes, to bring out the prisoners from the prison, and them that sit in darkness out of the prison house." Isaiah 42:6–7

13. "While Peter yet spake these words, the Holy Ghost fell on all them which heard the word. And they of the circumcision which believed were astonished, as many as came with Peter, because that on the Gentiles also was poured out the gift of the Holy Ghost. For they heard them speak with tongues, and magnify God. Then answered Peter, can any man forbid water, that these should not be baptized, which have received the Holy Ghost as well as we?" Acts 10:44–47

14. "In that day will I raise up the tabernacle of David that is fallen, and close up the breaches thereof; and I will raise up his ruins, and I will build it as in the days of old: Behold, the days come, saith the LORD, that the plowman shall overtake the reaper, and the treader of grapes him that soweth seed; and the mountains shall drop sweet wine, and all the hills shall melt. And I will plant them upon their land, and they shall no more be pulled up out of their land which I have given them, saith the LORD thy God." Amos 9:11, 13, 15

15. "Put ye in the sickle, for the harvest is ripe: come, get you down; for the press is full, the fats overflow; for their wickedness is great. Multitudes, multitudes in the valley of decision: for the day of the LORD is near in the valley of decision." Joel 3:13–14

16. "And it shall come to pass in that day, that the mountains shall drop down new wine, and the hills shall flow with milk, and all the rivers of Judah shall flow with waters, and a fountain shall come forth out of the house of the LORD, and shall water the valley of Shittim." Joel 3:18

17. "The Spirit of the Lord GOD is upon me; because the LORD hath anointed me to preach good tidings unto the meek; he hath sent me to bind up the brokenhearted, to proclaim liberty to the captives, and the opening of the prison to them that are bound; And they shall build the old wastes, they shall raise up the former desolations, and they shall repair the waste cities, the desolations of many generations." Isaiah 61:1, 4

18. "Therefore say unto the house of Israel, thus saith the Lord GOD; I do not this for your sakes, O house of Israel, but for mine holy name's sake, which ye have profaned among the heathen, whither ye went. And I will sanctify my great name, which was profaned among the heathen, which ye have profaned in the midst of them; and the heathen shall know that I am the LORD, saith the Lord GOD, when I shall be sanctified in you before their eyes. For I will take you from among the heathen, and gather you out of all countries, and will bring you into your own land. Then will I sprinkle clean water upon you, and ye shall be clean: from all your filthiness, and from all your idols, will I cleanse you. A

new heart also will I give you, and a new spirit will I put within you: and I will take away the stony heart out of your flesh, and I will give you an heart of flesh. And I will put my spirit within you, and cause you to walk in my statutes, and ye shall keep my judgments, and do them. Ezekiel 36:22–27

19. "Ye are my witnesses, saith the LORD, and my servant whom I have chosen: that ye may know and believe me, and understand that I am he: before me there was no God formed, neither shall there be after me." Isaiah 43:10

20. 2 "Notwithstanding the Lord stood with me, and strengthened me; that by me the preaching might be fully known, and that all the Gentiles might hear: and I was delivered out of the mouth of the lion. And the Lord shall deliver me from every evil work, and will preserve me unto his heavenly kingdom: to whom be glory for ever and ever. Amen." Timothy 4:17–18

21. "Let thy work appear unto thy servants, and thy glory unto their children. And let the beauty of the LORD our God be upon us: and establish thou the work of our hands upon us; yea, the work of our hands establish thou it." Psalm 90:16–17

22. "For God will save Zion, and will build the cities of Judah: that they may dwell there, and have it in possession. The seed also of his servants shall inherit it: and they that love his name shall dwell therein." Psalm 69:35–36

23. "I will hiss for them, and gather them; for I have redeemed them: and they shall increase as they have increased. And I will

sow them among the people: and they shall remember me in far countries; and they shall live with their children, and turn again." Zecharia 10:8–9

24. "And I will sow her unto me in the earth; and I will have mercy upon her that had not obtained mercy; and I will say to them which were not my people, Thou art my people; and they shall say, Thou art my God." Hosea 2:23

25. "If any man serve me, let him follow me; and where I am, there shall also my servant be: if any man serve me, him will my Father honour." John 12:26

26. "And Joshua the son of Nun was full of the spirit of wisdom; for Moses had laid his hands upon him: and the children of Israel hearkened unto him, and did as the LORD commanded Moses." Deuteronomy 34:9

27. "Who was faithful to him that appointed him, as also Moses was faithful in all his house. For every house is builded by some man; but he that built all things is God. But Christ as a son over his own house; whose house are we, if we hold fast the confidence and the rejoicing of the hope firm unto the end." Hebrews 3:2, 4, 6

28. "Even us, whom he hath called, not of the Jews only, but also of the Gentiles?" Romans 9:24

29. "Labour not for the meat which perisheth, but for that meat which endureth unto everlasting life, which the Son of man shall give unto you: for him hath God the Father sealed." John 6:27

30. "No man can come to me, except the Father which hath sent me draw him: and I will raise him up at the last day. It is written in the prophets, And they shall be all taught of God. Every man therefore that hath heard, and hath learned of the Father, cometh unto me. John 6:44–45

31. "Labour not for the meat which perisheth, but for that meat which endureth unto everlasting life, which the Son of man shall give unto you: for him hath God the Father sealed. Jesus answered and said unto them, This is the work of God, that ye believe on him whom he hath sent." John 6:27, 29

32. 2 "Who hath saved us, and called us with an holy calling, not according to our works, but according to his own purpose and grace, which was given us in Christ Jesus before the world began, but is now made manifest by the appearing of our Savior Jesus Christ, who hath abolished death, and hath brought life and immortality to light through the gospel." Timothy 1:9–10

33. "Whereunto I am appointed a preacher, and an apostle, and a teacher of the Gentiles." 2 Timothy 1:11

34. "So then neither is he that planteth anything, neither he that watereth; but God that giveth the increase. Now he that planteth and he that watereth are one: and every man shall receive his own reward according to his own labour. For we are labourers together with God: ye are God's husbandry, ye are God's building." 1 Corinthians 3:7–9

35. "As newborn babes, desire the sincere milk of the word, that ye may grow thereby:" 1 Peter 2:2

36. " For other foundation can no man lay than that is laid, which is Jesus Christ. Now if any man build upon this foundation gold, silver, precious stones, wood, hay, stubble; Every man's work shall be made manifest: for the day shall declare it, because it shall be revealed by fire; and the fire shall try every man's work of what sort it is. If any man's work abide which he hath built thereupon, he shall receive a reward." 1 Corinthians 3:11–14

37. "Now to him that is of power to stablish you according to my gospel, and the preaching of Jesus Christ, according to the revelation of the mystery, which was kept secret since the world began." Romans 16:25

38. "And he said, Therefore said I unto you, that no man can come unto me, except it were given unto him of my Father." John 6:65

39. "And this is the Father's will which hath sent me, that of all which he hath given me I should lose nothing, but should raise it up again at the last day. No man can come to me, except the Father which hath sent me draw him: and I will raise him up at the last day." John 6:39, 44

40. "For he that is called in the Lord, being a servant, is the Lord's freeman: likewise also he that is called, being free, is Christ's servant. Brethren, let every man, wherein he is called, therein abide with God." 1 Corinthians 7:22, 24

41. "We then, as workers together with him, beseech you also that ye receive not the grace of God in vain." 2 Corinthians 6:1

42. "But as God hath distributed to every man, as the Lord hath called every one, so let him walk. And so ordain I in all churches. Let every man abide in the same calling wherein he was called." 1 Corinthians 7:17, 20

43. "Fight the good fight of faith, lay hold on eternal life, whereunto thou art also called, and hast professed a good profession before many witnesses." 1 Timothy 6:12

44. "And he called his ten servants, and delivered them ten pounds, and said unto them, Occupy till I come." Luke 19:13

45. "Herein is my Father glorified, that ye bear much fruit; so shall ye be my disciples." John 15:8

46. "And ye shall know the truth, and the truth shall make you free." John 8:32

47. "And he fenced it, and gathered out the stones thereof, and planted it with the choicest vine, and built a tower in the midst of it, and also made a winepress therein: and he looked that it should bring forth grapes, and it brought forth wild grapes." Isaiah 5:2

48. "I the LORD have called thee in righteousness, and will hold thine hand, and will keep thee, and give thee for a covenant of the people, for a light of the Gentiles; To open the blind eyes,

to bring out the prisoners from the prison, and them that sit in darkness out of the prison house." Isaiah 42:6–7

49. "And other sheep I have, which are not of this fold: them also I must bring, and they shall hear my voice; and there shall be one fold, and one shepherd." John 10:16

50. "Even them will I bring to my holy mountain, and make them joyful in my house of prayer: their burnt offerings and their sacrifices shall be accepted upon mine altar; for mine house shall be called an house of prayer for all people. The Lord God, which gathereth the outcasts of Israel saith, Yet will I gather others to him, beside those that are gathered unto him." Isaiah 56:7–8

Prayer of Faith

Heavenly Father, I realize I have been a sinner; I committed these sins in ignorance, but now I have heard your Word, and I believe your Word of deliverance and life.

Today, I confess my sins and promise never to go back to them. Come into my heart (life) and save me unto eternity. Take absolute control of my life and glorify your name in me. I confess Jesus as my personal Lord and Savior. Wash me with the blood of Jesus, set me free, and transfer my name from the book of death to the book of Life. With my heart, I believe in your righteousness, and with my mouth, I confess that I am saved by the blood of my Lord Jesus.

Thank you for saving me in Jesus' mighty name, amen.

Covenant Steps to True Salvation

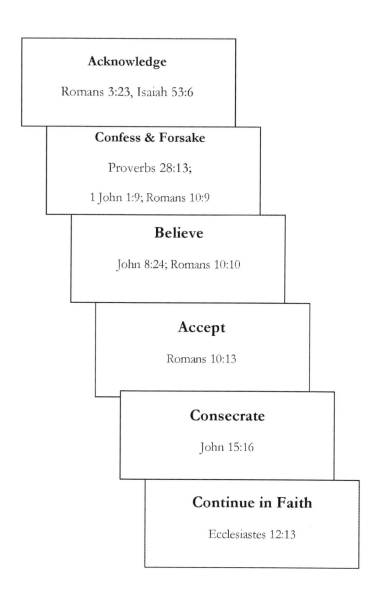

Acknowledge

Romans 3:23, Isaiah 53:6

Confess & Forsake

Proverbs 28:13;

1 John 1:9; Romans 10:9

Believe

John 8:24; Romans 10:10

Accept

Romans 10:13

Consecrate

John 15:16

Continue in Faith

Ecclesiastes 12:13

About the Author

Pastor Martins Ifeanyi Okonkwo is the presiding and end-time minister of All Nations Evangelistic World Outreach (ANEW), an apostolic, prophetic, and missionary ministry divinely commissioned to preach and teach the gospel of Jesus Christ around the world before the year of the Lord.

Martins is a conference speaker and a minister of the Lord with a burning passion for soul-winning.

Since his divine call in July 1995, when the Lord Jesus came to him, anointed him, and commissioned him to win souls globally for the kingdom of God, he has remained steadfast and consistent, always laboring in his vineyard. His contact with so many lost and unsaved souls has brought divine relief and restoration to them.

With the ANEW ministry and a prophetic declaration by the Lord, "You are a teacher of my Word across the world," the Lord intends to use him to bring revival to the body of Christ and in missionary assignments globally.

Martins holds a BA in theology from Temple College London and is currently rounding up his postgraduate degree in Christian theology at Heythrop College of the University of London.

He is happily married in the Lord to Oby C. Okonkwo.

Other Books by Martins Okonkwo

Pulling Down the Kingdom of Darkness

Hidden Keys to Divine Prosperity

Salvation—A Weapon against the Enemy

The Keys to Pleasing God

The Laws of Faith

Holiness: The Law of His House

email: matcom101@yahoo.com
facebook Address:
www.facebook.com/AllNationsEvangelisticWorldOutreachAnew

telephone: 447985422137